SHAKE YOUR TREE

SHAKE YOUR TREE

Memoirs of Marie Claire, Always Creole and Always a Proud Colored Former Slave Owner

PAULETTE FENDERSON HEBERT

Available for speaking engagements
paulette.hebert@cox.net
504-303-9746

iUniverse

SHAKE YOUR TREE
MEMOIRS OF MARIE CLAIRE, ALWAYS CREOLE AND ALWAYS A PROUD COLORED FORMER SLAVE OWNER

Copyright © 2021 Paulette Fenderson Hebert.

All rights reserved. No part of this book may be used or reproduced by any means, graphic, electronic, or mechanical, including photocopying, recording, taping or by any information storage retrieval system without the written permission of the author except in the case of brief quotations embodied in critical articles and reviews.

iUniverse books may be ordered through booksellers or by contacting:

iUniverse
1663 Liberty Drive
Bloomington, IN 47403
www.iuniverse.com
844-349-9409

Because of the dynamic nature of the Internet, any web addresses or links contained in this book may have changed since publication and may no longer be valid. The views expressed in this work are solely those of the author and do not necessarily reflect the views of the publisher, and the publisher hereby disclaims any responsibility for them.

Any people depicted in stock imagery provided by Getty Images are models, and such images are being used for illustrative purposes only.
Certain stock imagery © Getty Images.

ISBN: 978-1-6632-1900-8 (sc)
ISBN: 978-1-6632-2488-0 (e)

Library of Congress Control Number: 2021913712

Print information available on the last page.

iUniverse rev. date: 07/28/2021

INTRODUCTION

Someone must tell the whole story. How, one may ask, does the whole story differentiate from the present story? There is a misconception that the African American is monolithic in heredity, monotheism, philosophy, culture, aspirations, politics, and enslavement. My attempt is to show the often hidden side of enslavement. When you visit these areas that are not taught in school, you will see how some African Americans have a moral code and a frame of reference that is seldom spoken out loud but heard in hushed whispers. Sometimes the comments are not even made in English but in a French patois.

    I grew up in New Orleans, and I retired as a public school history teacher. I have always been knowledgeable and curious about history. When I attended public school, I was always allowed to catch a bus to go and spend time in the libraries of the various neighborhoods in which I lived. By various neighborhoods, I mean that my mother moved a lot. For example, I have had to enroll in six different elementary schools because of this fact. In the library, I loved to read biographies of famous people, read about the history of Louisiana, and of course, read about New Orleans. The strangest thing is that in all my reading, I never came across the type of information that I have discovered in researching this book.

    I sometimes wonder, "Why did I miss it?" Why, then, do a lot of people miss it? The troubling thing is that many people who are deeply involved have missed it, and some just know a small part, or they might have a "funny" feeling. This reminds me of the often-told story of baking a ham by first cutting off the two ends. Females of each generation of a family would begin baking a ham by cutting off each end. When someone would ask why this procedure was done, the only answer would be that Mama did it that way. Finally, someone found the oldest lady in the family and asked her did she cut off both ends of a ham before baking it. After replying yes, she was asked for her reason. First, she said that she had inherited all her grandmother's pots, cast iron skillets, and baking pots. Since the baking pot was too small to hold a whole ham, she cut off the ends, just as her grandmother had.

This matter was brought to my attention so many years ago by my first husband, Donald Esteen Senior, who said that his family had never been slaves. Of course, I, who was college-educated, denied his claim on all kinds of levels. I even accused him of being a snob by looking down on my people, who were from rural areas of Alabama and Mississippi. I just told him that all African Americans have the commonality of having been in bondage. After discovering in the twenty-first century that what he said years ago about his family was true, I had to apologize to him. I had to tell him about his family's story and some other families' stories and about how they were intertwined.

You see, he would be in the category of people who know just enough to know that they are different. He never had a problem, and no one in his immediate and near extended family had problems mixing with people of a darker hue.

On the other hand, by growing up in New Orleans, I learned early in my childhood that I could not follow every school friend home. In no uncertain terms, I have been called so many awful, vile names and told never to come and sit on their steps and never to play with their child by certain people of color because of my dark skin tone.

I remember a whole family that lived around the corner from my family in one neighborhood in the Upper Ninth Ward, on Feliciana Street, that would not even speak to me as I passed by, saying good morning or good evening. I don't know about most children in other cities and towns, but when I was a child, the parents' rule was that you had to speak to people every time that you passed them, even if you went that way ten times in one day. It only took one old lady on Cleveland Street to teach me a lasting lesson. She told my mama that I hadn't spoken to her the second time I passed her sitting on her steps. My mama gave me a whipping to last a lifetime because of what she said. That hurt me as a child that these people on Feliciana Street would not speak to me because I was dark.

I remember, especially, when I attended Valena C. Jones Elementary School in the Seventh Ward. The teachers would hit me with the wooden pointer or rulers on my knuckles for rule infractions and hit the lighter colored children on the palm of their hands for the same infractions. This is just one of the abuses I remember because of the color of my skin while attending school. Other examples of abuses included not being allowed to take messages to other teachers or to the office and not being allowed in the library club.

I doubt even the educators knew the real reason why they were making a difference in the school children. Like most people, they looked only at the skin color and thought that was the real difference. Some of them did not even know their own history. They did not know the real reason why they didn't like dark-skinned people who were the same race as they were. They did not know the real reason why they did not want their sons and daughters to date and marry dark-skinned people. This is what one would call practice and ritual without knowing the purpose.

What was the real purpose of the practice in Louisiana? If their family's lineage was traced, you would probably find these black people's ancestors owned slaves and plantations. To increase their holdings, they had to develop means to first protect what they had and then develop the best way to benefit the family, usually by arranged marriages to people who looked like them and brought equal or better assets to the table. So the root of the discrimination was purely economics and not skin color!

This is not the picture of slavery most of us grew up reading about in books. It was not the plantation system and owners Hollywood presented in movies, television programs, and documentaries. I have seen many, many movies about the Old South, with its Southern colonels and white ladies in hoop skirts. I have never seen portrayed people as dark as I am at a slave auction who were bidding on slaves.

When you shake the family trees in Louisiana, you will not find lily white but lots of black, brown, and tan. In the discussion of Marie Claire's family and her memories, these surnames are discussed: Allain, Andre, Arlent, Autreil, Balquet, Baril, Barralle, Barras, Barre, Barsconet, Baune Banne, Bayle, Bazile, Beauvais, Bebe, Belly, Bernoudy, Bertault, Bienville, Boire, Bonnette, Bordelon, Bouligny, Bourgeat, Breslin, Broyard Barre, Brule, Cadet, Cambrai, Caramouche, Cassaixolle, Cellier, Charbonnet, Charpentier, Chartra, Chassaignac, Chauvin, Chesse, Close, Couvillon, Daigle, Daunoy, de Beaulieu, de Charleville, de Gauvery, de la Freniere, de Lery, De Livaudais, de Montpelier, DeCoux, DeCuir, Decuire, Dehon, Dejean, Denis, Des Morriere, Deslonde, Desnoyers, Despalangue, Desrosiers, Destrehan, Domer, Domingue, Dreux, Dubuclet, Dubuclet d'Hauterive, Ducoyet, Dugue-Reuter, Dupas, Duperon, Duval, Falconer, Fazende, Fortin, Francour, Gajean, Gaspard, Gradenigo, Gravier, Gray, Gremillion, Guerin, Guillot, Higbee, Homard, Honore, Honore Destrehan, Hopkins, Hubeau, Jacquet, Jeansomme, Juge, Juneau, L'Arche, La Touche, Labbe, LaCour, Lafitte, Langlois, Latapie, LeBeuf, Lejeune, Lemelle, LePorche, Machado, Martin, Maury, Mayeux, Morgan, Nezat, Patin, Paume, Piedgars, Pierre, Poche, Pollard, Porche, Poree,

Portales, Portateie, Prevost, Provost, Purnell, Quevain, Quinton, Rabalais, Ricard, Riche, Robert, Roy, Rucker, Seldon, Sellier, Severin, Solomon, Tanneret, Tolbert-Gonzales, Tounoir, Toustou, Trepagmier, Trudeau, Verdier, Verret, Walters, Zeringue.

A few people have influenced me toward writing by giving me the needed encouragement. In the beginning was my mother, Mary Jane Perkins Fenderson, who taught me to read and write before I was old enough to attend public school. Through her examples of frequent storytelling about her family and her childhood, I was able to penetrate the mind, the cadence, and the vocabulary of an oral person who told her stories in details from memory. I would like to thank Mr. Hayes Milton Fields Senior, who encouraged me to write a book a very long time ago after reading one of my letters to his daughter Portia. I would like to thank Linda Brown, who gave me a table in her restaurant to begin writing this book. She also served me delicious food. Finally, I would like to thank Donald Esteen Senior, who encouraged me to write this book about his family.

Even though the persons depicted in this book are based on actual people, some of the characters are a blend of people and families. Some of the incidents are based on actual events, meshed events, and fictionalized events that reflect the period. Nevertheless, the characters, the families, their genealogies, and the histories will allow the reader to peep into the lives of Colored people who owned slaves and plantations.

CHAPTER 1

FIRST LIGHT, THE GENESIS

As a gentleman sauntered up the road with purpose, he ignored the fine black alluvial soil that covered his shoes and the bottom of his trousers. He was engrossed with breathing the fresh air into his nostrils. Although the non-polluted air was palpable, he did desire a cool breeze to come through. He was finally in Pointe Coupee Parish, which was nestled between the Atchafalaya and the Mississippi rivers. This countryside, though pleasant, was scorching. It was so hot that the inside of his nose burned from the heat. "It sure would be divine if there were some shade trees to sit under for a spell," he murmured to himself. "I am willing to wager these lands long ago lost the trees to men who farmed the land."

Unknown to the gentleman, he was being carefully observed by a gentle lady whom everyone called Miss Marie Claire. Miss Marie Claire sat on her porch and rocked her chair while sipping a tall glass of iced tea. On this particular day in 1890, she happened to look down the road, and she saw in the far distance a stranger making his way. As he came to a fork in the path, she thought, *I wonder if he will continue to my neighbor's house or if he will pass by here.*

By and by, he walked toward her, and he introduced himself. The gentleman said he was there to take a census of her family for the United States of America. This very young man showed his government identification and said he was from New Orleans. Why, Miss Marie Claire had not seen anyone from New Orleans since her fifth cousin Emelie DeCuir died and was funeralized there three years ago! So she asked him to sit and offered him some sweet tea. Amazingly, this tea tasted better than he had ever had at home.

After exchanging greetings, the census taker asked if some other family members were home this morning. Miss Marie Claire quickly answered no, everyone else was still busy doing farm work. Then the young man asked the older woman if she would allow him to ask the necessary questions for the census. Miss Marie Claire responded positively. It had been a long while since anyone had come to Lakeland in Pointe Coupee Parish to ask her anything. It was hard these days for an old lady to be listened to attentively. Her family was very tired of her talking about the glorious "old days" while they were now impoverished sharecroppers who no longer owned their own land.

He first asked her to name the head of this household. She answered, "My grandson, Louis Raymond Ricard, is the head of the family." At the age of 105, she was the oldest of the family who lived in the house. In fact, she thought to herself, she was the oldest member of her whole family. The next questions inquired about Louis's age, place of birth, and marital status. To those inquiries, she answered, "My grandson, Louis, is fifty-nine years old. He also was born in Pointe Coupee Parish. Louis' wife is named Hermina LaCour, and she is twenty-nine years old. She too was born in Pointe Coupee Parish."

She was asked next of her knowledge of the names and birth years of the children of this family. Miss Marie Claire's memory served her well enough to answer this question accurately. She began with the name and birth of the eldest Ricard child and worked her way down to the youngest one. "My great-grandchildren are named as follows: Bertha Anna Ricard (1875–), Joseph Petrum Cyprien Ricard (1877–), Ludovic Layton Ricard (1878–), Anna Ida Ricard (1881–), Sophie Cydalise Ricard (1883–), Linda Marie Ricard (1885–), Francis Raymond Ricard (1888–), and Josephine Olga Ricard (1890–)."

She politely revealed the other Ricard children's names and birth years. "My grandson's other children are named Theodore Raphael Ricard (1855–) and Athanas Alvarez Ricard (1857–)." When Miss Marie Claire was asked why there was such an age disparity between the latter two children and the ones that she named first, she was able to answer clearly, "These great-grandchildren were born to my grandson and his deceased wife, Josephine Bienville." After a short pause, the census taker informed Miss Marie Claire that he only needed information on persons who presently resided in the house. She nodded that she understood.

Finally, the young man asked her name and age. She answered, "My name is Marie Claire DeCuir, widow of Raymond Porche and Leandre Severin, who died in 1840 and 1862, respectively. Both my gentlemen husbands were rich Creole plantation owners. Mr. Porche, who was white, died before the beginning of the Civil War, and Mr. Severin, a free man of color, died in that war. He was a major for the Confederate States of America." She was so caught up in talking about her deceased husbands that she almost forgot to tell the young man that she was 105 years old, which she did.

The census taker looked at her to observe her skin coloring and the texture of her fine white hair. He mused to himself that this lady could pass for any old white woman he had seen. But he knew she lived on a Pointe Coupee Parish plantation that she shared with her sharecropper family, so she could not be a white person. So then he asked if she considered herself mulatto, colored, or black for the purpose of the census. She answered sternly, "I am certainly not black! I am mulatto by birth and Creole by culture."

Before the young man could express his confusion by what she said, Miss Marie Claire went into an involved explanation of herself. "I am a mulatto because my father was white and my mother was a free woman of color. My father owned a huge plantation in Pointe Coupee Parish. His name was Joseph Antoine DeCuir. My mother was Marie Francoise de Beaulieu. She was a free woman of color. Both of my parents were born in the 1700s, and they died in the 1800s. My parents had a spectacular social life during their life together on their plantation, which was called Austerlitz. It was called Austerlitz because of its association with Emperor Napoleon Bonaparte. The Creoles loved all things Napoleon.

"My siblings and I lived with luxury on our plantation. I had slaves to attend to my every need. In fact, my two personal slaves were named Felicite and Carmelite. Felicite, the mother of Carmelite, was born in the Congo, and she always struggled with the French language. However, Carmelite, who was born in Louisiana, had no problem communicating in Benue-Congo, French, and English. I have a particular funny tale to tell you about Carmelite.

"Sometimes, Carmelite would tease a particular temperamental goose with a stick. She thought that she could tickle the goose by sticking it with a branch under the wings. Instead, the goose would get angry and chase Carmelite around the yard. Since she feared getting pecked by the goose, Carmelite would always run up the woodpile. One winter day Carmelite did her regular routine of teasing the goose. The goose, of course, ran behind her in its defense. What Carmelite did not realize was that much wood had been removed from the pile because the winter was very harsh. The slaves had been slow in cutting wood to build up the woodpile to the previous day's height. So, when Carmelite ran up the woodpile, she was not high off of the ground. The goose, then, was able to get to her. Every time he pecked her little legs she would scream for Felicite.

"'Maw Maw! Maw Maw! Help me! Help Me! The goose is biting me all over my legs!' she screamed.

"Felicite was distraught when she heard the shrill screams of her baby girl. I think she cussed that goose out in her own language. Then Felicite snatched that goose by the neck and twirled it so hard the neck popped off, and that headless goose ran all around the yard until it passed out. All the slaves were outside watching the spectacle. But I tell you one thing: that goose sure enough made one fine meal for our family!"

The census taker was almost exhausted from listening to that explanation. "But," he stated, "your tale did not explain why you call yourself Creole. No person of color can call himself Creole! I have that information on the authority of leading historians Alcee Fortier and Charles Gayarre. I have read in their books that only white people who are descendants of French and Spanish colonists can call themselves Creole!"

Miss Marie Claire got irritated but not unnerved! She replied, "A Creole, by definition, is anyone—not just white people—who was born in the New World and was a descendent of either Spanish or French colonialists." As she had done many times before with other doubters, Miss Marie Claire began to recite her very proud Creole pedigree. This is her story.

"My fifth great-grandfather, Valerian Decuire, was born in Belgium in 1511. He had a son, Pierre Decuire, who was born in 1560 to an unknown mother in the same country. Pierre Decuire, my fourth great-grandfather, married Margarida Mendes Machado. She was born in 1574 in Belgium. Pierre Decuire and his wife Margarida had a son whom they named Simon. Simon Decuire was born in 1604. He married Jeanne Leufroy, and their son was called Simon Decuire Jr.

Born in 1641, he married Marguerite Dehon, who was born in 1645. This couple had my first great-grandfather, Albert Decuire, in 1673. Albert Decuire was my first great-grandfather who was born in France. He worked and lived in Belgium so he could be near his relatives. It was in Belgium that he met and courted the one who would later become my great-grandmother. Her name was Marie Catherine Jeanne Domer. Marie Catherine was born in 1673 in Belgium.

"Because Albert and Marie Catherine spoke French, they were allowed to emigrate from Belgium to France. Both of them hoped to save enough money for passage to Louisiana for the whole family. Meanwhile, my grandfather, Jean Francois Decuire, was born in 1704. They were considered French citizens now. In due time, the family emigrated from France to Louisiana. There, a French registrar dropped the final letter to our last name. It was no problem. No one wanted to make a fuss because they were glad to be allowed into Louisiana. When Jean Francois grew older, he married Genevieve Mayeux. Genevieve was born in 1727 in New Orleans. Neither Jean Francois nor Genevieve could neither read nor write. However, they were able with prompts to 'draw' their signatures on their marriage license.

"Would you believe that Jean Francois Decuire was thirty-nine years old when he became officially engaged to sixteen-year-old Genevieve Mayeux? The appeal to the Mayeux family was his extreme wealth. This pledge of marriage was done before a Notary of Pointe Coupee Parish by the name of Bernard Louis Patin on October 28, 1743. Both the future groom's parents and the future bride's parents, Pierre Mayeux and Marie Sellier, were present and were witnesses to the promise of marriage. Non-parent witnesses for the groom were Etienne DeCuir, Jacques DeCoux, Joseph Herbera, and Francois Allain. Those non-parent witnesses for the bride were Francois Mayeux, Pierre Ricard, and Jean Pierre Hardy, who was also called 'Laburge.' Everyone had to promise that the wedding would take place in a Catholic church.

On November 11, 1743, Jean Francois Decuire and Genevieve Mayeux were married in St. Francis Catholic Church, which is located in Pointe Coupee Parish.

These two persons were the parents of my father, Joseph Antoine DeCuir, who was born in 1752 in colonial Louisiana. So now, you see that I am a descendent of a French colonialist," said the exhausted Marie Claire DeCuir as she slowly poured herself some more tea from the pitcher.

"Pardon me for asking, but was your father, Joseph Antoine DeCuir, the first white DeCuir to take up with women of color and have children with them?" said the census taker. Miss Marie Claire heard his question but chose to ignore it then because she was tired and thirsty. She poured more tea for the both of them.

After sipping more tea, the census taker began to ask more questions. "What do you know of the Mayeux side of your family, ma'am? Is it as interesting as the relatives you have already mentioned?"

"I have been told a story that has not lost any details regarding my Mayeux family. Before I relate to you the amazing tale of my grandfather's survival skills, let me inform you about his beginnings. The first Mayeux on record was Francois Mayeux, who was born in Amiens, Somme Picardie, France, in 1670. He married Marie Breslin, who was born in Maintenay, Pas DeCalais, Picardie, France, in 1669. They both immigrated to Louisiana and purchased land to establish the Mayeux Plantation in Pointe Coupee Parish.

"On this frontier land, they lived in harsh conditions, in tents, while they cut down trees to develop the land and to build a home. Through hard work and determination, their sugar cane plantation was modeled after the other thriving plantations in the colony. There was, of course, a large house for the couple and their children. There were buildings for smithing, for carpentry, for sugar milling, for cooking, for educating, and for storage."

"Are those all the buildings?" he asked.

"Oh no!" she said excitedly. "I forgot to mention the barn! Anyway, as the children grew and matured, houses were built for them on land that was given to them by their parents. My great great-grandparents, Pierre and Marie died natural deaths on their plantation in 1747 and 1752 respectively.

"Their only child, a son, my great-grandfather, Pierre Francois Mayeux, was born in Amiens, Somme, Picardie, France on August 26, 1699. When he was twenty-one years old, he sailed with his parents to Louisiana on the ship *La Profond*. They arrived in the colony of Louisiana on September 20, 1720. Upon arrival in New Orleans, the parents began an urgent search for a suitable wife for their son. They did not want their young son to fall to fleshly vices and women of disrepute. They were able to contact some nuns who had just brought over a fresh batch of single young girls from France. The nuns brought information on a young girl whose name was Marie Francoise Sellier. Her surname was actually Cellier, but the misspelling continues to this day.

"When Marie Francoise Sellier was born in 1707 in the same home town as Pierre Francois Mayeux, her father, Jean Cellier (1665–), was forty-two years old, and her mother, Anne Cadet (1676–1734), was thirty-one years old. He married Anne Cadet on June 27, 1693, in France. Jean Cellier's father was Pierre Cellier, who was born in 1625 in Beziers, Herault, France. Pierre Cellier married Francoise Barralle in 1654. She was born on August 20, 1628, in Lodeve, Herault, France. Francoise Barralle's parents were Antoine Baril (1600–) and Francoise Cassaixolle (1610–). Anne Cadet's parents were Antoine Cadet (1646–) and Marie Toustou (1660). They lived in Belcaire, Aude, France.

"In 1719, at the age of twelve, young Marie Francoise Sellier's parents allowed her to travel with a group of young single girls to the New World. This group of like-minded young ladies sailed as a group with the sole intention of finding suitable husbands. These young ladies, mind you, were not allowed to run loose. They were chaperoned under the watchful eyes of several nuns. In due time after their arrival in 1720, the girls were soon married. You see, the single suitable eligible men far outnumbered these young white girls. Among the men who were looking for brides was Pierre Francois Mayeux.

"My great-grandfather Pierre Francois Mayeux married Marie Francoise Sellier in 1720. They worked hard on the plantation that Pierre's family purchased. Sometimes later, he took my great-grandmother away from his parents' plantation to make his own way to the Arkansas Fort. The Arkansas settlement was a part of the Louisiana Colony at that time. He loved adventure and the rugged life. He sought to find his independent fortune there. While they were settled in the Arkansas Colony, their first child was born. His name was Francois Pierre Mayeux, who was born in 1723.

"Following the birth of their first child, my great-grandparents moved their small family to a better trading place, which was the settlement called Natchez. The colony of Natchez sat on a large bluff and looked over the Mississippi River. In fact, Natchez sat so high that if there were no trees to obstruct the view and if a person had telescopic vision, a person could look down on New Orleans from Natchez.

"In the colony, my great-grandfather was a trader and a driver. He had business dealings with the French settlers and the Indians. My great-grandmother even had the pleasure to take a trip to New Orleans where, she could have her second child in comfort. Genevieve Mayeux was born in the city of New Orleans during the year of 1727. Two years after my great-grandmother Marie Francois returned to Natchez with baby Genevieve, something awful happened!"

"What happened?" inquired the census taker.

"Everything seemed to be going well for a while. However, some scandalous colonists stole some furs from the Indians during 1729. Because they had not been compensated and because this was not the first theft, the Natchez, the Yazoo, and the Chickasaw Indian tribes banded together to exterminate the whole white settlement. They actually won the fight because they outnumbered the French settlers. Almost everyone, men, women and children were slaughtered. All the little brooks and small bodies of waters that flowed into the Mississippi River ran red with spilled blood. Human carcasses were on the ground, where they were savagely attacked and eaten by animals. No one received a Christian burial of the remains.

Only two men and their wives and their children were spared their lives. They were allowed to survive provided they followed two instructions the Indians gave. First, they had to leave immediately, and second, they could not take anything with them. You have guessed correctly if you thought my great-grandfather and my great-grandmother were some of the survivors. Other persons spared were their friend LeBeau and his wife. I don't know about LeBeau, but my great-grandfather was always fair with his dealings with the Indians. He never cheated them. Often he would extend credit to them for food and supplies when they had nothing to trade because of the harsh winters. Nevertheless, my people had nowhere to go but home to the Mayeux Plantation in Pointe Coupee Parish."

"Did your great-grandparents, the Mayeuxs, live happily on the plantation after the Natchez Massacre?" asked the census taker.

"Yes, they did!" shouted Miss Marie Claire. "Yes, in contrast to the uncivilized rugged life that they lived in the Arkansas and Natchez colonies, they became involved in the social activities in and around the large cities and the small towns. They enjoyed reading current newspapers, wearing nice clothes, eating well, being served by slaves, and attending and hosting fancy parties. Also, they had three more children.

"Their second daughter, Cecile Mayeux, was born in 1729, when Genevieve was two years old. Cecile married Jean Louis Homard on

April 18, 1747, in Pointe Coupee Parish. She was eighteen years old when she died on December 17, 1747, which was the same year she was married. Cecile did not have any children. Madeleine Mayeux (1733–03/27/1758) was the third daughter who was born. She married Joseph Provost on April 5, 1749, in the home parish church. They had five children before she died at the age of twenty-five on their Provost Plantation.

"The last child my great-grandparents had was Marguerite Mayeux, who was born in 1735. She first married Antoine Patin on June 2, 1749. Antoine was born on the Patin Plantation in 1727, in Bayou Goula, Iberville Parish. Unfortunately, he died on December 28, 1770. After his demise, Marguerite married another wealthy planter, from St. John the Baptist Parish. His name was Guillaume Andre LeBeuf (01/11/1746–12/09/1824). They married June 29, 1774. Marguerite died June 29, 1774. Even though she married twice, Marguerite had no children.

"The only son of my great-grandparents was Francois Pierre Mayeux (1723–1765). He married a French immigrant whose name was Nicole Prevost (1729–09/22/1765). They were married on the Mayeux Plantation on February 11, 1745. They lived together in their own big house on the Mayeux Plantation. Nicole died at the very young age of thirty-six, after having six children.

"As for my great-grandparents, my great-grandmother Marie Francoise Sellier died at the age of thirty-two in 1739. She had been married to my great-grandfather Pierre Francois Mayeux for nineteen years. My great-grandfather died eight years later, in 1747, at the age of forty-eight."

"Ma'am, please tell me some more of Genevieve, who would become your grandmother," stated the young man.

"Oh, yes! Genevieve Mayeux did grow up and marry my grandfather Pierre Francois DeCuir. These two were the parents of my father, Joseph

Antoine DeCuir. My grandfather died in 1771, and Genevieve died in 1779. She was left with the awful responsibility of managing the DeCuir Plantation and its financial holdings.

"In 1779, a smallpox epidemic raged through Pointe Coupee Parish. Unfortunately, Genevieve came down with the disease. She traveled to New Orleans to seek professional medical attention. The diagnosis was fatal, and the sickness made her weak very fast. However, she had the presence of mind to provide for her three minor children in a last will and testament. In her will, she left specific instructions for their care. These minor children were Jean Pierre DeCuir (10/04/1761–02/06/1827), Antoine DeCuir (10/04/1765–02/06/1827), and Jean Baptiste Dorsin DeCuir (12/30/1769–05/29/1860). Genevieve named Jean Baptiste Tounoir, her son-in-law, as the guardian of her three children. When Jean Baptiste Tounoir was twenty-eight years old, he married Genevieve Mayeux and Jean Francois DeCuir's fifteen-year-old daughter, Marie Anne DeCuir (10/21/1758–11/30/1805) on June 21, 1774, in St. Francis Catholic Church in Pointe Coupee Parish."

"What became of these three children?" asked the census taker.

Miss Marie Claire began to answer his question by saying, "Jean Pierre DeCuir was 18 years old at the time of his mother's death. He married Charlotte Julie Labbe on October 31, 1781. They didn't have any children. He died on February 6, 1827, in New Orleans, at the age of sixty-five. Antoine DeCuir was fourteen years old when his mother died. He neither married nor had any children. Antoine died on February 17, 1829, at the age of sixty-three. When Jean Baptiste Dorsin DeCuir was ten years old, his mother passed away. He married Helene Bourgeat on May 30, 1799, in Pointe Coupee Parish. They had seven children in thirteen years. He died of natural causes on May 29, 1860, on the DeCuir Plantation at the impressive age of ninety!"

The young man had become engrossed in Miss Marie Claire's story with amazement. It seemed her eyes lit up and the years peeled from her face as she spoke and explained each generation of her family and how they were tied to France. Even he would have had trouble trying to memorize and recite his generations. They were known to him only as names of births, baptisms, marriages and deaths that were recorded in the family's Bible. He requested a refill in his tea glass.

"So then, Miss Marie Claire, you said your grandmother Genevieve Mayeux, on her deathbed, bequeathed guardianship of her three minor children to her son-in-law, Jean Baptiste Tounoir Jr.?" asked the census taker.

"Yes, she did," said Miss Marie Claire.

"Well, who was he, and what kind of family did he come from?" inquired the young man.

"Jean Baptiste Tounoir Jr. (1755–03/04/1798) was chosen by my grandmother to guide the affairs of her three minor children because he was literate and a man of good moral standing. He came from a family that had a good reputation. Because the Tounoir family was wealthy in its own right, she trusted that her son-in-law would not be greedy and steal her children's inheritance. Genevieve also believed him not to be a wasteful gambler who would take unnecessary risks with what she was leaving her children.

"My father's sister Marie Anne DeCuir (10/21/1758–11/30/1805) married into a family that had its roots in France. The first Tounoir that I heard about was Jean Baptiste Tounoir Sr., who was born in 1730 in Poitiers, Vienne, Poitou-Charentes, France. He married Jeanne Bazile (1733–), who lived in France also. Jean and Jeanne emigrated from France to Louisiana. They settled in Pointe Coupee Parish on land that they purchased and had cleared for the first of several plantations that would be owned by the future powerful Tounoir family. Jean increased his wealth by growing products that were suitable for the climate and the landscape. He grew cotton, sugar cane and sweet potatoes. Jean died at the age of seventy-nine in 1809. His wife Jeanne died soon afterward.

"When Jean Baptiste Tounoir Jr. was born in 1755, his father, Jean Sr., was twenty-five and his mother, Jeanne, was twenty-two. Jean Baptiste Tounoir Jr. was born during the year when there were wars among the French, the Indians, and the American colonists. Most history books call it the French and Indian War.

"Before his marriage to Marie Anne DeCuir, Jean Baptiste Tounoir Jr. had a son with a free woman of color. I don't know her name. However, the son's name was fmc Jean Pierre Francois Tounoir (1758–1848). This Jean Pierre had a daughter whose name was fwc Artemise Tounoir (1817–). No one knows Artemise's mother's name or whether she was a slave or a free person of color. Artemise had a son, whom she named fmc Ursin Tounoir. He was born in 1842 on the Tounoir Plantation. Artemise never revealed the name of her son's father.

"Excuse me, madame," interrupted the census taker, "but I have noticed in my interviews of other people in this area, some Colored people want to have the appellation fwc or fmc in front of their names. Since I didn't understand the reason, I did not write it. I feel comfortable enough with you to ask, why do you use the terms and what do they mean?"

"In the simplest terms that you can understand, sir, fwc means free woman of color, and fmc means free man of color," answered Miss Marie Claire.

"But, ma'am, said the young man, aren't all Colored people free now?"

"Yes, you are right," answered Miss Marie Claire. "But you see, those three letters in front of somebody's name allow others to know they are looking at a person who probably was never a slave and that the person came from an important family. Do you see what I mean?" asked the elderly lady.

"Yes, I do," he said. "Please continue with your story."

"Well, let me go on. These are the children of Jean Baptiste Tounoir Jr. and Marie Anne DeCuir. They were all born in Pointe Coupee Parish.

Their first child was Francois Tounoir, who was born on October 17, 1775. For some unknown reason, the baby died the same day that he was born. Second to come was Jean Baptiste Bernard Tounoir (08/20/1777–01/30/1842). Their first daughter was Marie Helene Tounoir, who was born on March 6, 1779, and died on December 29, 1808, when she was only twenty-nine years old. On September 12, 1780, Joseph Tounoir was born and he died on March 6, 1836, when he was fifty-five years old. Genevieve Tounoir was born in 1782, and unfortunately she also died on the day of her birth of unknown circumstances. Born on November 12, 1784, was their son Martin Tounoir. He died on September 12, 1847. The birth of son Cyprien Tounoir was a third catastrophe for the parents. Little Cyprien was a live birth in 1787, but later during the same day he was born, he passed away. Next to be born was Marie Lucille Tounoir on December 13, 1789. Marie Lucille died on May 5, 1820, when she was thirty years old. Then Eusebie Tounoir was born on March 16, 1796. At the age thirty-five, she died on October 5, 1831, after she attended my daughter's wedding in the same year. Their last child that was born was Marie Desiree Tounoir, who appeared on August 14, 1798, which was five months after her father died at the age of forty-three. Marie Desiree died on her plantation in West Baton Rouge Parish in 1848.

When my cousin, twenty-three-year-old Jean Baptiste Bernard Tounoir, was ready to marry, he could not find any suitable white ladies for a wife, so a marriage contract was brokered between him and thirty-year-old fwc Aimee Porche. They were married on her parents' plantation in Point Coupee Parish on February 28, 1810.

"Pardon me, ma'am. Please tell me why he married someone who was seven years older than he was," the census taker anxiously asked.

"I'll be delighted to explain the reason behind the marriage. It was a matter of an economic move of combining assets, sir. Aimee Porche was the daughter of the wealthy planter Vincent Alexis Porche and fwc Adelaide Caramouche," explained Miss Marie Claire.

"So, her parents were mixed?" he asked.

"Yes," said she.

"Tell me about the parents, please," pleaded the census taker.

"Vincent Alexis Porche and fwc Adelaide Caramouche had a long-term loving relationship. During this relationship, thirteen children were born. The children were born when their parents were not married. In this culture, the parents not being married did not make a difference in the children's last name. Neither did it affect their inheritance and their reputation. Everything the children needed had been legalized by a notary. They were accepted on all levels of society with the Porche name. These children were looked at as being very acceptable for marriage because they had the required pedigree and wealth. Why their names show up as foreparents of many prominent Louisiana families in the highest strata of polite society! Their names were fwc Aimee Porche (1780–1855), fwc Julie Porche (1797–1831), fwc Cydalise Porche (1799–), fwc Azelite Porche 1802–), fmc Alexis Reine Porche (1804–1887), fmc Hypolite Porche (1807–), fwc Eugenie Porche (1808–1827), fwc Helene Porche (1810–1868), fmc Martin Porche (1811–1861), fwc Adelaide Porche (1813–), fwc Euphemie Porche (1813–), fwc Euchariste Porche (1818–), and fmc Leonard Porche (1820–). Nevertheless, after the last child was born, Vincent Alexis Porche and fwc Adelaide Caramouche were married on the Porche Plantation in 1829.

"The first child who was born to my cousin Jean Baptiste Bernard Tounoir and fwc Aimee Porche was fwc Eugenie Tounoir, who was born in 1808 in Pointe Coupee Parish on the parents' Tounoir Plantation. All her siblings were born there too! Eugenie married her sixty-two-year-old uncle, Alexis Porche, when she was eighteen years old in 1826. Alexis Porche was her uncle because he was the son of her grandparents, Vincent I. Alexis LePorche and Marie Francoise Pauque Poche. The

SHAKE YOUR TREE

couple received a dispensation from the priest of St. Francis Catholic Church to marry each other. A year after the wedding, at the age of nineteen years old, she died! Eugenie Tounoir never had any children.

"Jean Baptiste Bernard Tounoir and fwc Aimee Porche's only son was born in 1811. His name was fmc Martin Tounoir. He died on the Martin Tounoir Plantation at the age of fifty in 1861. Martin never married, and he had no children.

"A second daughter who was born to the couple was fwc Helene Tounoir in 1810. At the age of thirty-nine, Helene married twenty-seven-year-old fmc Francois Gabriel 'Florville' Bouligny. Francois was born into the prosperous Bouligny family on October 5, 1812, in Plaquemines Parish on the Bouligny Plantation. The wealth of the Bouligny family was known by all people everywhere. This family had accumulated their financial holdings by successfully merging with the Fazende and Charbonnet families by marriages.

"The first record that I know of the Fazende family began with Jacques Antoine de Fazende, who was born in 1677 in France. I don't know exactly when he arrived in Louisiana. He married twelve-year-old Helene Des Morriere in 1708 in New Orleans. Jacques was thirty-one years old at the time of his marriage. Helene Des Morriere was a native of New Orleans. They had eight children in twenty-six years. They were all born in New Orleans. The wealth of this Fazende family came as a result of smart banking skills as well as being able to successfully make stock market decisions on Louisiana produce and stock.

"Jean Rene Gabriel Fazende, at age thirty-eight, married Charlotte Constance Dreux, who was fifteen years old. They were married in New Orleans on April 14, 1760. They had eighteen children in their thirty-nine years of marriage. Charlotte died in 1835. Jean Rene Gabriel Fazende died a long time ago, in 1799."

"Is there much more?" the tired young man interjected.

"Do you want me to continue my story or not?" Miss Marie Claire defiantly asked.

"Yes, please go on," said the census taker in a subdued voice.

"Well, I am going to connect the background of the Fazende family with my family. Just bear with me, please," she said calmly. "The third child of Jean Rene Fazende and Charlotte Constance Dreux, Jean Gabriel Fazende (1762–1808) married fwc Constance Eulalie L'Arche sometimes during 1798 in New Orleans. Together, they owned a vast amount of land acreage that was located on their own Fazende Plantation in Jesuit Bend that was located in Plaquemines Parish. Only thirty slaves worked the land by 1800. The Fazendes felt pity for a poor blind white man and hired him to do some menial tasks. To show you how strange they were, they even employed eight free males of color who were employed as carpenters, smiths, and chief wranglers. I tell you, sir, this was not a good idea," said Miss Marie Claire in anguish.

"Why, shouldn't freemen of color be hired for pay? Weren't they trustworthy?" asked the census taker.

"Young man, you don't know what you are talking about," said the elderly lady. "That's like putting an eagle next to your caged pet canary. You see, it's not a good idea to mix free workers on plantations with slaves because free black people could come and go as they wish, and they had to be paid for their work. It was far better for slaves not to see other black people working for money. It could cause disharmony, disenchantment, and rebellion.

"Permit me, sir, to name the children of Jean Gabriel Fazende and fwc Constance Eulalie L'Arche. Perhaps they may sound familiar to you. Their first child was fwc Antoinette 'Ana Maria' Fazende, who was born on February 24, 1787. She died on August 16, 1864. Their first son was fmc Francisco Fazende, who was born sometime during 1794. He passed away on August 20, 1876, which was a few years ago. A second daughter, fwc Celeste Arsene Fazende, was born on April 15,

1798. She died when she was a young girl. Twin daughter's fwc Eulalie and fwc Anne Fazende were born around 1802. Anne passed away on June 28, 1853, at the age of fifty-one years old. It is not known when Eulalie died. When the twins were two years old, another daughter, fwc Constance Fazende was born on March 24, 1804, and she lived a long life of seventy-five years. She died on March 8, 1880, which was ten years ago. Then, three brothers followed her birth. One was fmc Jean Pierre Azenor Fazende, who was born on the Fazende Plantation in Plaquemines Parish during the year 1808. He died sometime in 1854. Another brother was fmc Hugo Fazende, who was born on November 3, 1814.

"Then there was the brother who married into my Charbonnet family. His name was fmc Gabriel Theodore Fazende, who was born in 1810. He married fwc Alexandrine Charbonnet (1815–06/14/1873). Alexandrine was born on the Charbonnet Plantation in St. Charles Parish, which belonged to her father, my cousin, wealthy planter Jacques Charbonnet (02/1770–03/25/1837) of France and her mother, fwc Alexandrine Melanie Bernoudy (01/01/1783–04/30/1841). Her parents were married on the Charbonnet Plantation in 1807.

"The oldest child of Jean Gabriel Fazende and fwc Constance Eulalie L'Arche was able to unite the wealth of the Fazende family and wealth of the Bouligny family by marriage. Her name was fmc Antoinette 'Ana Marie' Fazende. She married Francisco Josef Ursino Ursin Bouligny. His Bouligny Plantation was located at a place called English Turn in Plaquemines Parish. She lived the rest of her seventy-seven years in opulent luxury, with plenty of slaves to wait on her, slaves to grow the crops, slaves to take care of the animals, slaves to clean the house, slaves to cook the food, slaves to transport her in her wagon, and slaves to nurse the babies.

"They had six children and raised them on their plantation in Plaquemines Parish. Their first born was fmc Francois Gabriel "Florville"

Bouligny, who was born October 5, 1812. He died on October 10, 1874, at the age of sixty-two years old. Their first daughter was fwc Marie Louise Bouligny, who was born in 1815 and died in 1867. The second son was fmc Dominique Ursin Gabriel Bouligny. He was born during 1817, and he passed away sometime in 1851. Three more sons were born in this order: First was fmc Louis Gabriel Bouligny in 1821, and he died in 1837. Second was fmc Victor Clement Bouligny who was born in 1826. I think that he is still living. Last to be born was fmc Gabriel Constantine Bouligny, and I know he is still living.

"When fmc Francois Gabriel 'Florville' Bouligny was born in English Turn, Plaquemines Parish, his father, Francisco, was thirty-three, and his mother, fwc 'Ana Maria,' was twenty-five. On April 16, 1839, fmc Francois Gabriel 'Florville' Bouligny married fwc Helene Tounoir in her parents' Jean Baptiste Bernard Tounoir Plantation in Pointe Coupee Parish. I would not have missed the wedding for anything but a sickness to death! I know what kind of money my relatives had. I knew the wedding was going to have a lot going on and that everyone would be happy and satisfied with the accommodations, the amenities, and the food. However, I knew it was not going to be as grand as the wedding I gave for my daughter in 1831. I was right too! All of our immediate family, some of our extended family, and dear friends were present. But I must say, there were not as many in attendance as at my daughter's earlier wedding. The parents of the bride were there. They were fwc Aimee Porche and Jean Baptiste Bernard Tounoir. Of course, the grandparents of the bride were there. They were my father's sister Marie Anne DeCuir and her husband, Jean Baptiste Tounoir Jr.

"'Florville' and 'Ana Marie' divided their time during their marriage between the Bouligny Plantation in Plaquemines Parish and the Tounoir Plantation in Pointe Coupee Parish. They had four children during their marriage. Their names are as follows: fwc Marie Antoinette Bouligny, who was born on December 29, 1841. Second to be born was fmc

Francois 'Frank D' Bouligny, who was born on September 29, 1844, while they were visiting Terrebonne Parish. He is still living. The third child born was fwc Ema Bouligny, who was born on June 22, 1846. She died as a teenager in Hermitage, Pointe Coupee Parish in 1861. The last child born was fwc Virginia Bouligny. I do not know when she was born, and I do not know if she is still living.

"In the meantime, fmc Francois Gabriel 'Florville' Bouligny had a parallel family with a mistress and children that were born during the time his wife was having her children. They all lived together on the same plantation but in different mansions. The mistress's name was fwc Medorine Pierre, who was born in 1823 in Pointe Coupee Parish. She died in the early part of 1880. She had a total of nine children with Francois. These nine children were all born on the Bouligny Plantation. The names of these children are as follows: fwc Cecile Bouligny (1852–), fmc Andre Andrew Bouligny (1854–), fwc Amelina Amelia Bouligny (10/13/1857), fmc Paul Bouligny (1860–04/27/1868), fmc Moise 'Moses' Bouligny, fmc Edgard Bouligny, fwc Eugenie Bouligny (02/22/1867–), and fmc Abraham Bismarck Bouligny (11/27/1870).

"What is amazing to me is that fwc Medorine Pierre and fmc Francois Gabriel 'Florville' Bouligny married in a quiet ceremony the very day that his first wife died, which was on October 8, 1874. I am at a loss for words over the matter. You would have thought that they would have at least waited until she was buried in the ground!

"I must tell you that the family of my aunt, Marie Anne DeCuir, did not escape even more public humiliation among the people and in the courts. Another child of hers was the subject of a vicious scandal. This was Joseph Tounoir, her fourth child. You see, sir, in a parish as small as Pointe Coupee, it is impossible to carry on an adulterous affair without his wife's knowledge. In most cases out here, the wife usually stood her ground and maintained her position in the marriage. However, this was not the case for my cousin, Joseph Tounoir. On May

27, 1805, Joseph married Rosaline Porche (03/29/1790–08/1859) in Pointe Coupee Parish.

"Rosaline Porche came from a very prominent and wealthy family with a prolific pedigree! In other words, she was an excellent catch. She was someone who could expand her husband's holdings. She was the granddaughter of Vincent I. Alexis Le Porche and Marie Francoise Pauque Poche, first, of France and then Ponte Coupee Parish. Her parents were Alexis Porche (1764–) and Europhosine Riche (1773–1830). Her father, Alexis Porche, was the same one who received a Catholic Church dispensation to marry his niece, fwc Eugenie Tounoir, in 1826. Rosaline's upstanding siblings were Zenon Porche (1792–1861), Villeneuve Porche (1795–1834), Vergara Porche (1799–1860), and Delphine Elisabeth Porche (1802–1845).

"On August 5, 1827, Rosalind Porche filed for divorce! This move of hers went against the expectations for the usual wives in Louisiana. She had good grounds and proof for her case. She even produced witnesses during the court proceedings that verified her husband was having an adulterous affair with fwc Fannie Riche. The Parish of Pointe Coupee granted Rosaline a divorce on May 24, 1828. Rosaline was successful in her divorce petition because she employed a skillful attorney who was able to have her walk away with half of her husband's land, animals, slaves, and money.

"Now, this fwc Fannie Riche was the natural and declared daughter of the planter Frederick Riche. Although Fannie was her father's slave at her birth in 1805, she grew up to be a fine-looking young girl. Well, the sultry-looking Fannie caught the eye of Joseph Tounoir one day as he visited the plantation of Frederick Riche. Immediately when he saw her, he began swooning with all kinds of imaginations with her.

"For a good price, he purchased Fannie from her father, who was also her owner. He made Fannie one of his house slaves. But her only job was to pleasure her new owner at his will. To make it more convenient for him, he gave Fannie one of the upstairs bedrooms in the main house. Oh, he was very, very pleased with Fannie! Because of their differences in age, Joseph thought Fannie would outlive him. He wanted to be sure Fannie would not be still a slave at his death and suffer harsh beatings from his wife Rosaline. So, he bargained with Fannie for her freedom.

"In exchange for her freedom, he asked her to remain on the plantation and to take care of him until he died. Of course, she agreed, and Fannie received her papers of manumission on August 24, 1823. These papers were also filed in the Pointe Coupee Parish Court House. Both this living arrangement and freedom of Fannie Riche infuriated his wife, Rosaline Porche.

"Joseph Tounoir passed away on March 16, 1836, with no apparent heirs. He did not have any children. So, Rosalind and other family members sued each other very publicly and angrily for the Joseph Tounoir Plantation. However, to everyone's surprise, Joseph left a registered notarized last will and testament! In it, he said that after all his debts were paid, his land, house, buildings, slaves, animals, and money were to be given to fwc Fannie Riche. Rosaline and the family contested the will in the courts. In fact, they appealed all the way to the state supreme court. The final court upheld the validity of the will. Everyone now calls the Joseph Tounoir house the Fannie Riche Mansion. She lives there today, and she is over ninety years old.

"Another Tounoir family of note was Martin Tounoir. Martin was the sixth-born child of my aunt Marie Anne DeCuir and Jean Baptiste Bernard Tounoir Jr. During a slave auction in Pointe Coupee Parish, his attention was focused on a very attractive twenty-year-old mulatto whose name was Lydia Seldon. The slave auctioneer and her owner, a Mr. John Maury, stated that her nickname was 'Lady.' She was called 'Lady' because of her natural gracefulness, charm, ease of movement, and attractive features.

"Immediately, Martin Tounoir knew he had to purchase 'Lady'

for himself at any price. Well, he paid the hefty sum of seven hundred United States dollars to own her on December 29, 1806. No one came close to his bid!

"'Lady' was born on the John Maury Plantation in Tennessee in 1786. It is said, but he never admitted like most Americans, that 'Lady' was John Maury's natural child. Martin and 'Lady' had eight children before they were married. Their names were fwc Celanie Tounoir (1807–1847), fwc Euphemie Tounoir (1809–1847), fmc Martin Tounoir Jr. (1810–), fmc Alexandre Tounoir (1812–), fmc Eleuthere Heluter Tounoir (1814–1879), fwc Marie Leda Tounoir (1816–1872), fwc Lucille Tounoir (1825–), and fmc Jean Baptiste Tounoir (1826–1869).

"Martin Tounoir and fwc Lydia 'Lady' Seldon were married on April 21, 1841, on the Martin Tounoir Plantation in Pointe Coupee Parish. 'Lady' died on December 30, 1844, and she was buried in the cemetery of St. Francis Catholic Church. Later her husband, Martin Tounoir, was buried next to her after he died on September 12, 1847. Martin never remarried after the death of his wife. His children by 'Lady' inherited his Tounoir Plantation because they were his only heirs."

CHAPTER 2

AS GOOD AS IT GETS

After he concluded drinking his last glass of tea, the young man continued to write information on the census form. As he approached the line for the race of the other family members in the home, he became puzzled.

"Should I check mulatto for the rest of your family too?" he said.

"Oh no!" exclaimed Miss Marie Claire. "I am the only one who can be called a mulatto in this house. My dearly departed daughter, Cydalise Celenie Porche, the mother of my grandson, Louis Raymond Ricard, was a quadroon. Louis and his wife would be called octoroon on your paper," she said.

"Hum," groaned the young man, "those classifications are not listed here!"

"Well, now!" Miss Marie Claire said. "Check them off as being colored because they are not black and they are not white either." Then she said, "I need to educate you as well as your employer about us. I don't know if they really care about Creole people! A mulatto has one parent who is of the African race. A quadroon is one-quarter African. An octoroon is one-eighth African. And a quintroon is one-sixteenth

African. I learned these names of people from my mother. It is too bad the government did not know this information for you to do your job properly," Miss Marie Claire said excitedly.

It was becoming late in the day as the sun was beginning to set. The census taker had not finished his assignment because he had become so intrigued with the elderly lady and her stories. Because there were no hotels around, he would have to sleep outside under the stars. He really did not gravitate to the idea of sleeping outside because he was afraid of the wildlife. He was truly a city boy who had known the comforts of living in the city all his life.

Shortly, the household members began to return home from farming as sharecroppers. They farmed the land for the owner for wages and a home in which to live. They hardly ever had a lot of money to show for their work after harvest time. Some years they broke even and did not make any money for the year. It was then that they had to ask for credit at the owner's store to buy goods, which included food, clothes, shoes, and seeds for the winter and for the following year. Fortunately, they were allowed a piece of land for a family garden. They worked from sunup to sundown, farming for the owner. They worked in their own garden during weekends.

Because they were very poor, they needed all adults and physically able children to work the fields. Sending the children to school was not even considered. Because of their poverty after the Civil War, the adults did not like hearing or even speaking about the family's wealth before the war. This is why they did not like listening to Miss Marie Claire's stories about the arrival of their white families to Louisiana and the marriages and cohabitation of the free women of color to these wealthy white men. Now they had to work hard for the white man to survive.

Miss Marie Claire said to her grandson, "Louis, this young man is from New Orleans. He works for the government in Washington. He is here to ask us questions for the census."

"How do you do, sir?" said Louis.

"I am well, sir. Uh, Mr. Ricard, sir, I am pleased to make your acquaintance," the census taker said nervously.

After the family washed the dirt from their faces, arms, and hands, the young man gathered his nerves together to make an appeal to Louis Raymond Ricard.

"As head of the house, Mr. Ricard, sir, I beg and I plead with you to give me shelter for only one night. If you could just spare a small corner of a room to sleep for the night on the floor, it would please me very much. I promise not to take up much room, sir," he begged.

The tired and hungry Mr. Ricard replied, "Being poor and not having a lot of room was not a reason to refuse hospitality." He pointed to the floor and said, "Find a good spot to make yourself comfortable."

Mr. Ricard yelled at the children, "Somebody get our guest a blanket so he can make a pallet on the floor!"

Then the family and the guest sat down at the table to eat. After the food was blessed, everyone ate the rib-sticking meal that had been prepared by Miss Marie Claire. They laughed and talked loudly as they ate the delicious meal. Finally, the dessert was served. It was fluffy vanilla custard. They ate all the food.

After the meal and the cleaning of dishes, the family sat around the light of the coal oil lamp and laughed at the wild animal stories told by the parents. The guest also smiled at the tales of the animals. It seemed to him the animals in the stories got into similar situations as did humans. He was amazed that those animals could plot and conceive of 'evildoing' just as humans did. They even had the same desires as humans, which were to enlarge their territories by either stealing other animals' lands or by sending their young ones to mate with older animals.

As the story telling stopped, the census taker inquired of Mr. Ricard if his father's family came from either France or Spain.

"My father's family came from France," he responded.

"Interesting," said the census taker. "Did the Ricard family arrive in Louisiana a long time ago?" inquired the young man.

"Yes, my second great-grandfather, Pierre Ricard, was the first Ricard to arrive in Louisiana in 1718. This was the founding year of the city of New Orleans by Bienville. It was also during the Colonial Period of Louisiana. He was born in 1702 in the city of Aquitaine, France. Although his parents, Jean Ricard, who was born in 1676, and Marie Bayle, who was born in 1680, were not wealthy, Pierre earned his money through trading in futures of goods that arrived from Asia. Because Pierre found favor within the court of the king and with the king's minister of colonial affairs, he was given a healthy land grant in Louisiana. The land that was given to him was located near the fort in Pointe Coupee Parish."

"I do know that the area of Point Coupee Parish as well as the other rural areas of Louisiana was sparsely populated during the Colonial Period of Louisiana," said the census taker. "So then, Mr. Ricard, how did Pierre Ricard find labor to cut down the trees and remove the tree stumps for him to have a productive plantation?" he inquired.

To answer that question, Mr. Ricard began to assemble, in his head, the story that had been repeated to him very often. In fact, this oral tale had been told to all the Ricard families over several generations. The story even had a name. It was called the "Story of the Beginnings."

"I will now tell you the story of how the first Ricard Plantation developed from forest and swamp land and how our family grew," stated Mr. Ricard. "It all started with the explorer Jean Baptiste Le Moyne, Sieur de Bienville, and his crew of free African sailors and their families!" exclaimed Mr. Ricard.

"One day in 1718, Bienville asked some of the African men to complete some work for him. Bienville asked them to accompany him to lower Louisiana, which is now Plaquemines Parish, with the mules to release a log jam in the waterways. To assist them in their assignment, the men brought hatchets and ropes with them.

"First, they stripped the branches of the logs with hatchets while they simultaneously straddled the logs. Then they tied one end of each rope to a mule, and they tied the other end of the rope to each log. To separate the logs, the men carefully guided the mules in the shallow part of the water. What these men forgot was that a horse will work until he dies, but not a mule. It seemed that within seconds of each other, all the mules sat down in the water, refusing to pull the logs that were attached to the ropes. Well, the logs kept moving and smashed into the mules. The mules were killed instantly.

"Bienville cared more about his mules being dead than the welfare of the men. So Bienville, without a pause, ordered those men to be whipped with a hundred lashes. Not liking the idea of being whipped like common slaves, these men, one and all, grumbled, mumbled, stretched their eyes, and had air in their jowls. But not one of them said a word. They knew their place with the white man.

"However, their body language was an insult to Bienville, as it would have been to any white man. Bienville sold those angry African men along with their families to my second great-grandfather Pierre Ricard (1702–1773), who was now a wealthy Louisiana land owner who desired to have a large productive plantation.

"By the way, Bienville released the rest of the African crew and their families from his boats to settle in the colony as free persons. He gave them their salaries and supplies. My second great-grandfather was pleased with the purchase of these slaves because he needed to raise enough cotton, indigo, and beans to sell as cash crops so he could afford to have the hand in marriage of the lovely Marie Louise Desnoyers (1729–1773) of Natchez, Mississippi. Her family were natives of France by way of Quebec, Canada.

"It was on January 7, 1745, that Pierre Ricard, age forty-three, married Marie Louise Desnoyers, age twenty-two, in St. Francis Catholic Church in Pointe Coupee Parish. Pierre Ricard and Marie Louise Desnoyers had these children, Antoine De Rieutard Ricard (–1815), Marie Francoise Ricard (1745–1814), Charlotte Julie Ricard (1748–1808), Edne Ricard (1750–1750) and Pierre Ricard, Jr. (1747–1750).

"Their oldest son, Antoine De Rieutard Ricard, married a free woman of color, Marianne dite Ricard (1738–1819) of Jamaica. Her Jamaican parents were also named Ricard. Her parents, the white planter Joseph Ricard (1716–) and a free woman of color, Anne Jacquet (–1766) had a plantation in that English colony. Antoine and Marianne lived on one of the Ricard Plantations in Pointe Coupee Parish. There, they happily raised crops and children. The names of these children were fmc Agicole Ricard, fwc Claire Ricard, fwc Hortense De Rieutard Ricard, fmc Pierre St. Luc Ricard (1758–1814), fwc Adelaide Ricard (1769–1850), fmc Cyprien Ricard (1783–1826), and fmc Maximilian Ricard (1786–1823). Because the parents were racially mixed, their children were free persons of color. In legal documents and in conversations, the males were addressed as 'fmc,' or free man of color and the females were addressed as 'fwc' or free woman of color.

"Allow me to tell you about the family of Antoine De Rieutard Ricard and fwc Marianne dite Ricard's son, fmc Pierre St. Luc Ricard. In 1804, the son of Antoine De Rieutard Ricard and fwc Marianne dite Ricard, fmc Pierre St. Luc Ricard married a free woman, Marguerite Marie Antoinette Belly (1786–1846) in Bayou Goula, Iberville Parish. Iberville Parish was the place of her birth. The father of fwc Marguerite Marie Antoinette Belly was Pierre Belly (1738–1814) who was born in Blaye, Gironde, Aquitaine, France. Her mother was Marie Rose Belly (1758–1828), a free woman who was born in Jamaica. The children of Pierre St. Luc Ricard and Marguerite Belly were the freemen of color, Pierre St. Luc Ricard IV (1805–1886) and Antoine St. Luc Ricard (1813–1873).

My father, fmc Pierre St. Luc Ricard IV, married my mother, free woman of color Cydalise Celenie Porche (1816–1862) in 1831. I am the eldest child. I was born in 1831. Before you ask me, I will tell you I came from a very large family. My parents had twelve children. My siblings are named fmc Joseph Aristide Ricard (1834–), fwc Lodoiska Ricard (1838–), fmc George Samuel Santa Anna Ricard (1848–), fmc Palmyr Luc Ricard (1835–1837), fwc Marie Estelle Ricard (1840–), fmc Pierre Hilarion Ricard (1842–), fmc Antoine Rudolph Ricard (1850–1882), fwc Alicia Claire Regine Ricard (1853–), fwc Marie Eliska Ricard (1857–), fmc Sacerdos Israel Ricard (1845–), and fwc Philomena Elizabeth Ricard (1857)."

"Mr. Ricard, as freemen of color, did your age-eligible brothers and you feel compelled to fight the South in the Civil War to free other black people?" inquired the census taker.

"Are you crazy?" shouted Mr. Ricard. "Why should we have fought on the Yankees' side? The slaves were our property! They were our birthright! Nobody, I mean nobody, had a right to take our property! Those damn Yankees wanted to take our slave property away from us! Who was going to work our land? With the price of cotton and other crops going up and down in the market, we could not afford to pay people to work our lands, tend to our animals and babies, to cook our food, to clean our houses, to clean our clothes, and to dress our bodies. Why, whatever would we have done without our slaves?

"So, yes sir, mister census taker, my four age-eligible brothers and I proudly put on the Confederate gray uniform to fight to maintain our heritage and our way of living. Ask somebody who knows our people, such as a priest. If my word is not good enough, ask a priest about us. He will tell you how the Church along with the organization enabled our free people of color to achieve our possessions and our positions in society. A priest will testify to you that we had been high on the social ladder right next to white people since Colonial Louisiana, through the Antebellum Period and the Civil War. Now, since the war is over, and after the so-called Reconstruction Period, we have lost all of our property and our social status. Our people are similar to wounded animals that go away while they wait to die! Sir, we don't identify ourselves with those former slaves now, after the war, especially since we lost all our plantations and homes. We are Creole! They and their kind could never be equal to us because we were never slaves, and we used to own them! We don't even mix with them socially since the war in any kind of way. One of those darkies had better not look at one of our silky white skin daughters to talk about courting them. Like I say, they need to marry their own kind!"

"Mr. Ricard, that very long exaltation leaves me puzzled with some questions to ask," said the census taker. He then said, "I know that most of the free black people from the North and from the South fought in their own colored infantries for the Union. They said they wanted all black people to be free so that they could work for wages like all the other people. I don't think that they even thought that they would have opposing black people as your brothers, other free black people, and you fighting them in the Confederate uniform. In fact, most black people from the North had the idea that if they would see black people in gray uniforms, those people would have been under forced servitude to wait on their masters. They even thought they were probably assigned jobs away from the front lines, such as munitions caretakers, cooks, porters, nurses, latrine diggers, and grave diggers. So, Mr. Ricard, could you calmly explain to me, as simply as possible, why free black persons like you supported the Confederate States of America?" inquired the census taker.

"Sir," said Mr. Ricard, "I am not responsible for the allusions that all Northerners and any people thought about free black people fighting for the South. I actually feel sympathy for their misconceptions. We had our all black militia, and some of us gallantly served with white people. We were there fighting for Louisiana. To think that no black person would fight against their "saviors" is a misunderstanding of our circumstances. You see, sir, free black people of color in Louisiana owned slaves on plantations in rural parishes such as Pointe Coupee, Iberville, East Baton Rouge, West Baton Rouge, St. Charles, St. John the Baptist, Avoyelles, Plaquemines, St. Landry, Natchitoches, West Feliciana, and others and in the city of New Orleans. Therefore, there was a vested interest in keeping the slavery system for the slave-owning black man as well as the slave-owning white man. It was purely a case of economics. Free labor is always better than paid labor. Now, that's all it is, sir!"

"Oh, I see now," said the census taker. "Please, tell me, Mr. Ricard," said he, "what part did the priests pay in your group of people's economic and social status?"

"You see, sir, answered Mr. Ricard, since Louisiana was first explored by men such as Rene-Robert Cavalier, Sieur de LaSalle and Pierre Le Moyne, Sieur d'Iberville a priest always accompanied them along with free Africans. The priests were there to make all non-Catholics, Catholic. Africans were with them because of their knowledge of telling directions by using the stars at night. The Africans were very skilled in astrology, and they studied the stars intensely. As I stated previously, free Africans were with Iberville's brother, Jean Baptiste Le Moyne, Sieur de Bienville.

"During those periods, the priests got acquainted with those African men and sometimes with their families. Those priests explained to them that the only religion allowed in France and all French colonies was Roman Catholicism! Those free Africans were informed that they had to be baptized as Catholic converts if they wanted to live as free people in the French colonies. They found them to be of good moral character and easily converted them from Islam to Catholicism. Most of the

Africans were allowed to settle in Louisiana during the Exploration and the Colonial periods.

"Then, during Louisiana's Colonial Period and for a time during the Antebellum Period, there was a shortage of white women to marry. So, it was not unusual for a French immigrant and his sons to marry or cohabit with either slaves or free women of color and sometimes Indians. If you thought women were rare in New Orleans, they were scarcer in rural Louisiana on the plantations. A rich planter not only needed a wife; he needed legal heirs. Even against some civil laws, priests, at the request of plantation owners, would approve marriages between planters and free women of color. If the rural planter only wanted to cohabit with the free woman or the slave, the priest would then baptize the children of the union with the father's last name. They would then become his legal heirs with the stamp of approval from the Church." After this explanation, Mr. Ricard became very tired. "Is that the last question?" he asked the census taker.

"Oh, no, I have one more inquiry of you," he said.

"Okay, what is your question?" asked a very tired Mr. Ricard.

"You mentioned that the organization played a part in the social and financial success of free black people. What was the organization? What were its goals? How were they accomplished?" inquired the census taker.

"My, my, that one more question was big enough and long enough to choke a big-mouth goat," said Mr. Ricard. "Sir, the situation in all of colonial Louisiana was a desert as far as the availability of white women to marry. In New Orleans, a custom began in the form of quadroon balls and octoroon balls. These balls had nothing at all to do with the functions and purposes of the organization. But I will tell you of these balls so you can compare and contrast those activities with those of the organization. For the balls, a group of free women of color would rent a ballroom to introduce their daughters to wealthy colonial Frenchmen and later wealthy colonial Spanish men. These women hoped their daughters would become mistresses to these important men. After the proper introductions were made between the young ladies and the men, they usually danced, talked politely and sipped on punch, and ate little food. After a young lady received the attention of a particular gentleman for a while, her fate was usually sealed.

"The next step was for the gentleman to contract with the mother on the terms of the daughter's placement. This placement of the daughter was called a placage, and she was the placee. The contract had agreements on monthly contributions to the daughter and the mother, a purchase of a town house for the daughter, slaves to run the home and to provide her comfort and education in France for the children. Now, most contracts did not provide for the placee after the death of the benefactor. Finally, the children did not benefit from his name, and often, they were omitted from his will as heirs.

"Now then, let me tell you about the organization. First, the organization focused on where the need for women were in most demand and where the wealthy men were most generous. From the beginning of the Colonial Period, the rich French and Creole planters in rural Louisiana were desperate for women. The freemen of color who were descendants of the families of the free Africans that arrived with the explorers were organizers and members of the organization.

"They knew that these French and Creole men were honorable men. Didn't they allow them and their families to remain free? These honorable men were willing to claim their seed, the children, by sharing their surnames, their lands, their slaves, their wealth, and their influences. Rules were very few in the organization. Everyone was admonished never to reveal the members of the organization to outsiders, commonly known as Perpetrators.

"Let me explain who the Perpetrators were. They were freed slaves who tried to enter the membership ranks. Why would the organization allow people who had allowed themselves to be enslaved in the organization? They had no pedigree! Members knew not to write down anything, so everything had to be remembered and recited.

"Once there was a silly member of the organization who befriended a former slave who was skilled in iron work. This former slaver worked for the member in his iron work business that molded and installed the kind of ornate iron galleries that you see on the French Quarter buildings. This employee had five daughters whom he wished to marry wealthy planters. The member made the mistake of introducing one of the daughters of the former slave to a very good prospect.

"Because he talked the organization's business and introduced the young lady to one of the planters who had been spoken of in an Organization meeting, he was hunted down viciously at night by men on horseback, had his tongue split, and was left on a trail to die. The punishment for talking and writing about any business of the organization was to have the tongue cut out of the mouth!"

"Excuse me, Mr. Ricard, sir, but why weren't the daughters made available to the men in New Orleans for marriage?" exclaimed the census taker.

"The reasons should be obvious, mister census taker," said Mr. Ricard. "In New Orleans, the daughters did not have the same respect, social status, wealth, and the family surname as the white gentleman. Another thing, sir, the gentlemen of the city gave the placees an allowance for herself and her mother. The placee used the money for her personal needs. She hardly had enough money left over to provide for other family members, especially her brothers. Food and milk were delivered to her home, fresh daily and paid by the gentleman. She did not have to pay for housekeeping and duties around the townhouse because he supplied an ample amount of slaves. The education of their children by private tutors was paid by him also. If she desired her sons to have further education, their father sent them to a European boarding school of higher education. Their daughters were sent to a boarding finishing school in Boston.

"Now, let me further explain the situation. Our daughters were taught to share the wealth with their families, especially their brothers. Society prohibited the free brothers of color to marry or cohabit with rich white women. But they could, however, rise to the top economically on the successes of their sisters. Just as water seeks its own level, the children of these unions were taught to marry on their own economical level. Love was not an issue. If love became an issue, the girls were placed in a Catholic convent and made nuns, and the boys were banished to Texas or further west.

"Eventually, another goal of the organization would be to have their descendants placed in all the rich and powerful families in rural Louisiana plantations. To accomplish that goal and to keep the money in the family, uncles were allowed to marry nieces and first cousins were allowed to marry each other. To make those consanguineous marriages possible, the priests' permission was sought. Usually, the parties received the blessings of the priests and the priests had the parents of the bride and groom sign a contract. Sometimes these contracts were made when either or both parties were infants. It was a matter of money, you see, and keeping it in the family. Their motto was 'money grows money.'

"Last but not least, sir, all of our generations had strict instructions from their parents and the organization never to pity the plight of slaves. It did not matter if slaves were the same color as we were or if they had been freed; they were still just niggers—that's all! If truth be told, sir, we treated our niggers worse than white masters. You know why? We never wanted slaves to think that just because we were the same color, they could slack on all the work that had to be done on the plantations."

"Excuse me for interrupting again, sir," said the young man. "But what would have happened before the Civil War if a man such as yourself took up with a slave or a former slave, put her in the mansion, and treated her like a lady?" inquired the census taker.

"Simply put, he would have been shunned by his family and his neighbors," shouted Mr. Ricard. "However, the children from that union would have been accepted simply because children are innocent and heirs are still needed to expand the boundaries of the plantation and to keep the name going. See, that's looking at the big picture. Now, mister census taker, I will go to sleep," said Mr. Ricard.

CHAPTER 3

CHASING THE GOOD LIFE

During the second day, the census taker had an extended conversation with Miss Marie Claire. She was bursting all over to resume talking to him about her family. It was such a joy to have someone so intensely waiting to hear her every word. "Miss Marie, you have been here over one hundred years," said the census taker.

"To be exact, sir, it has been one hundred five years," answered Miss Marie Claire. "As a matter of fact, sir, I am probably the only person who you will count in your census that has lived through Louisiana's Colonial Period, the beginning of statehood, the Antebellum Period, the War of 1812, the Mexican War, the Civil War, and the Reconstruction Period. Sir, just like Louisiana, our free families have risen and fallen in similar cycles. It's similar to the rise and fall of the Roman Empire."

"What did you mean by that last statement?" asked the census taker.

"Well, you see, during Louisiana's Colonial Period, the men and slaves cleared the land for the colony for settlement on the plantations in the rural parishes such as Pointe Coupee, Iberville, St. Landry, Avoyelles, West and East Baton Rouge, and the German Coast. By the time Louisiana was a state, the plantations were populated, and trade had begun.

"During the Antebellum Period, trade for cotton and other produce was at its height. And if you want to know what we were doing, I will tell you. We were consumers of every kind of material thing imaginable. We had all our wants met. Then came the Civil War. We fought gallantly for the South for the ideals we held dearest to our hearts. Many of our boys were proud officers for the Confederacy. Some died valiantly, others returned as heroes, and some had crippled bodies and minds. Meanwhile, on the plantations, we nearly starved during the war. The Yankee soldiers took all our livestock to feed their soldiers and we were kept on our knees as beggars without food. The Yankees did not allow us to keep our crops to eat and take to markets. Instead, they burned our crops that were still in the ground and in the barns.

"After the South lost the Civil War, we lost our way of life. Even though the period was called the Reconstruction Period, it was not a time of reconstruction for former plantation owners. Since then, we have had to work in the fields for the new owners to keep food on our table."

"But, Miss Marie Claire, what exactly happened to your money, your plantations, and your way of life?" asked the census taker.

"Don't you understand, sir, about what happened?" asked Miss Marie Claire. "I told you that the livestock had been taken away and the crops had been burned! Think about it, sir! The war released our free labor, the slaves! So if we had nothing to sell and no labor to work the fields, how could we get new money?"

"New money?" questioned the census taker.

"Yes, sir, new money. The old money had been stashes of worthless Confederate money. We needed some Yankee dollars. Because we lacked Yankee dollars, we could not pay our real estate taxes and assessments. As a result, all the rural parish governments made the tax collectors auction our land, furniture, and clothes to others. Now to have sufficiency for life, our men and ladies have to work the fields as slaves used to do."

"Oh my, Miss Marie Claire! I have never heard of these things going on with people of color," exclaimed the census taker. "Please continue. I am most interested in the manner you and the people of color conducted yourselves during your youth before all the problems came with the Civil War."

"Sir, I want to inform you of some things that few people know about or want to acknowledge. It may seem odd to some folks that free people of color in Louisiana had wealth, influence, respect, and slaves," said Miss Marie Claire.

"Hmm," said the young man in almost disbelief.

"Well, this is Louisiana, isn't it?" she said with a raised voice. "This state was always different from the rest of the United States. You know that this state has political divisions of parishes and not counties as do the other states, right? Also, our laws are not based on common law but the Napoleonic Code, right? Louisiana's differences practically confound most out-of-state people. The harsh laws and practices that governed free people of color in other states regarding behavior, curfews, work, banking, burial, interracial marriages, and dress did not exist in Louisiana as a common practice. Why, if a free person of color had enough money, he could enjoy all the benefits of most white men!" she explained.

Continuing, Miss Marie Claire stated, "Unlike Colonial American slave owners, the rural French Creole and French immigrant planters acknowledged their children from slaves, Native Americans, and free persons of color. I tell you, sir, it was no wonder that free women of color and slave women gladly—I mean gladly—submitted to those Frenchmen and French Creole plantation owners in rural Louisiana! They knew of the long run benefits for the children of these relationships.

"Those children received education either in France or by private tutors. Included in the rights of our free people of color of the plantations were the rights to address the courts, testify against white people, sue, and be sued. Nobody in my day could say our people were shy and reclusive. The opposite was true. We were bold, colorful, and boastful people.

"As far as being wealthy, Cyprien Ricard had more money than any free person of color in the whole world. Our wealth was seen in our opulent lifestyle. For example, our ladies had personal modistes. No money was held back in purchasing rich cloths for making clothing. Encouraged by the latest styles in Paris, our clothes were made of satin, silk, and embossed cotton. Of course, the modistes embellished the outfits with imported handmade lace. Each outfit had accessories of matching hats, parasols, handkerchiefs, and gloves.

"Often, we ladies along with our chaperones were seen riding in closed carriages with a driver and our personal slave. Ah, but our male relatives could be seen riding on horseback. No carriages for them! They loved to show off their tailored riding clothes while they galloped on the roads and in towns with their beautiful stallions and engraved saddles."

"Ma'am, all of these amazing tales about the lives of the colored slave owners sound good. What about the plight of your slaves? Were they happy also?"

"They should have been happy! Every Sunday, they were given a day off to attend Mass at St. Francis Catholic Church," exclaimed Miss Marie Claire.

"So, Miss Marie Claire, are you trying to say to me your slaves, who worked six days a week from before dawn to dusk and were given one day a week to attend church, never dreamed or talked about being free?" asked the census taker.

"Well … yes. A few times, there were uprisings, but they were squashed either by the family members or the state militia," she said.

"However, I do remember a very enormous slave revolt that

happened around 1811. In fact, that revolt began right here in Pointe Coupee Parish on my father's plantation. It seems that the slaves from various plantations had been meeting secretly at night in the deep woods on my father's land. You would have thought that we would have been alerted by the sight of lit lanterns. But you know those crazy niggers met in the woods without any light! I tell you, I don't know how they did not bump into each other or fall into a bayou with the alligators.

"But one night, I was up using the pot in my bedroom, I heard the rear door open and shut, and then, I heard some footsteps. I yelled, 'Who goes there?'

"'It is me,' a small timid voice answered.

"'Carmelite, is that you?' I inquired.

"'Yes, ma'am, it is me,' she said.

"'Pray tell, what are you doing coming into the house at this time of morning? I want the truth!' I said.

"'Well, you see ...' she stuttered.

"'No! No! No! Carmelite, I know you like the back of my hand. When you begin your explanations with "Well, you see," I know you are getting ready to tell me a lie!' I screamed.

"'Ma'am, I have been going to meetings,' she said shyly.

"'Who is having meetings? Where are these meetings? What are they talking about in these meetings?' I drilled her.

"'Ma'am, the slaves have been meeting in your father's woods. They come from all over! I don't know exactly what they are talking about because I get confused with the languages in my head. Sometimes I think that I am hearing French, and at the same time, I think I am hearing English. So I don't know what to tell you. Please, ma'am, that's all I know,' she said with tears going down her face.

"'Well, Carmelite, that is all right! I will tell my father about these meetings on his property. What I want you to do is to keep attending these meetings just as you have been doing and keep your ears open. It is your duty to me as my personal slave to report anything that you hear that would disrupt the peace of our plantation. Haven't I always been good to your mom and you?' I asked.

"'Yes, ma'am, you have always been good to us. I will do just as you asked me to do. If I hear something that will disturb our peace on our plantation, I will bring it back to you,' she said.

"Now, mister census taker, it did not take a long time for the plans of the slaves to become known to us. With Carmelite faithfully working on the inside, we obtained information they planned a slave revolt on all the plantations in Louisiana, which would begin in Pointe Coupee Parish. The plan was that once the slaves found out what happened in Pointe Coupee, all Louisiana slaves would use that as an example and revolt all over the state. In the plans they even conceived of the idea of burning all the plantation homes and murdering all planters and women and children.

"So my father and the other planters armed themselves and sent someone to get the state militia for protection. Because we knew the exact date, which was January 8, 1811, and the place the slaves would revolt, we were able to arm ourselves and to inform the militia. This militia consisted of white men and our sons. I tell you, sir, it was not easy to put the slaves down. Even though we had better weapons, they were armed with superior courage. However, in the end, our men were able to eliminate the slave revolt in Pointe Coupee Parish. As a punishment and as an example to other slaves, the slave bodies were hanged on trees along the River Road from Pointe Coupee Parish to New Orleans!"

"Was that all to the revolt? It doesn't seem as though a lot went into planning it, and it doesn't seem as if enough people were involved to be a great threat to anyone!" said the census taker.

"No, no, no, sir!" shouted Miss Marie Claire. "That was the only part that Carmelite knew about and could give a report. What she didn't know was how extensively the slave revolt was planned. At the same time as the slaves were acting out in Pointe Coupee Parish, close to one thousand slaves were revolting in St. Charles Parish and St. John the Baptist Parish. I have learned since then that their plans were to recruit slaves up and down the River Road and to murder all of the white and colored planters, their wives, children, and loyal slaves. The ultimate goal was to murder and burn all the way to New Orleans and do the same to all of its citizens who were not slaves. I heard they were not going to even give sympathies to any free person of color because they viewed all of them as potential slave owners."

"Wow! It's hard to believe that ignorant slaves could think of such a brilliant but horrible plan!" exclaimed the census taker. "I am glad no one was harmed!"

"Oh no, sir, you are mistaken! People were killed, harmed, and evacuated from their homes. Those slaves were armed with small pistols, cane knives, and kerosene bombs!" said Miss Marie Claire.

"Ma'am, what is a kerosene bomb?" asked the young man.

"Well, imagine any small metal or glass container that you could hold in your hand. The slave would put some kerosene in it and place a cloth wick in that container. Then they would tie rags around the top so the oil would not spill out. When the slave would spot his target such as windows of houses and hay in barns, he would light the wick from a blazing torch, aim, and throw at his victim's house or his victim's barn."

"So, who was hurt or killed?" asked the census taker.

"Unfortunately, the Maurice Trepagnier family, on its plantation, in St. Charles Parish, was hacked to death. They even killed the planter's small children and an infant. All the buildings were burned down. I don't remember the names of all the families who were slaughtered, but according to what people say, there were quite a few.

"As the crowd meandered through St. Charles Parish, the slave rebels thought they were freeing the slaves so that their rebellion numbers would increase, so the slaves were allowed to live. However, a few loyal slaves went ahead of the mob to warn the planters who lived on the River Road about the impending danger that was on its way.

"Fortunately, my distant cousin Jacques Philippe Charbonnet (1770–1837) and his wife fwc Alexandrine Melanie Bernoudy (1783–1841) and their children were warned in time to leave the plantation with their children for their safety. It was not even a burden to him to carry his elderly crippled mother, Marie Antoinette DeLivaudais (01/05/1745–1812), out of the home on his back!

"They and the other planters, both white and colored, united and hunted the slave rebels with guns and dogs. The riot was put down because the plantation owners had superior weapons. Riders had been sent to the state house. Governor William C. C. Claiborne then sent a militia with orders to hang all the participants in the nearest trees."

"My, my, this is an interesting tale. I never learned about the Slave Revolt of 1811 in school," he said.

"There are a lot of things you probably haven't heard about in school," she replied.

"Miss Marie Claire, everything about your family is so intriguing with all of its twists and turns," remarked the census taker. "But even with all the schemes, scandals and such, it seems everyone in your family remained on the right side of the law," he commented. "But seriously, ma'am, did you ever have any crooks or law breakers in your family?" inquired the census taker.

"Well, yeah, umm there was one occasion when there was a plot for murder, a trial and an execution," answered Miss Marie Claire.

"Well, do go on ma'am," encouraged the young man.

"It began with Marin Chauvin who was born on March 16, 1625, in Tourouvre, Orne, France. He was the son of Nicholas Chauvin (1593–) and Catherine Piedgars. Both of his parents were French citizens also. Marin Chauvin left France and arrived in Quebec, Canada, in March 23, 1648, at the young age of twenty-three. While in Quebec, he met

Gillette Marie Baune Banne in a town in Quebec called Trois Rivières. Gillette Marie was originally from Caen, Calvados, France, where she was born in 1636. Her parents were Marin Baune Banne (1590–1651) and Isabelle Boire (1592–1648). Isabelle Boire married Marin Baune Banne in Boyeux, Calvados, France, in 1620 when she was twenty-eight years old.

"Gillette left her parents at an early age and sailed to Quebec, Canada with an aunt and uncle and some cousins. Her mission was to find a suitable husband who owned his own land. She did not want to be poor. The only way to get out of the economic level that she was born in was to leave France and to seek her fortune in the New World. She arrived in Quebec, Canada, with her family in 1649.

"It did not take a long time for Gillette Marie Baune Banne and Marin Chauvin to meet each other. Through the introduction of his friends and the inspection and approval of the aunt and uncle, a marriage contract was drawn up for the young people. It was posted in the local Catholic Church. The reason why it was posted in the church was to give people a chance to object to the marriage. For example, either one of the engaged persons could have had bad character traits such as violence, laziness, gambling, thievery, or another spouse. After an appropriate lapse of time, Marin Chauvin, age twenty-four, and Gillette Marie Baune Banne, age thirteen, were married in Trois-Rivières, Quebec, Canada, in 1649, which was the same year as her arrival in Quebec.

"On September 8, 1650, their daughter, Marie Chauvin, was born. She was their only child. The house was filled with joy! However, this joy was short-lived. The husband, Marin, passed away on June 5, 1651, in Trois-Rivières, Quebec, Canada, at the age of twenty-six years old. They had been married two years.

"Gillette was an experienced widow who was old enough now to meet men and make her own marriage accommodations. She then met and later married Jacques Bertault (1626–1672) in Trois-Rivières,

Quebec, Canada, on July 27, 1653, when she was seventeen years old. They had six children during their marriage. The names of these children were Jacques Bertault Jr. (1655–1667), Marguerite Bertault (1655–1687), Suzanne Bertault (1657–1739), Elisabeth Therese Isabelle Bertault (1659–1736), Jeanne Bertault (1660–1698), and Nicolas Bertault (1662–1672). All of the children were born in Trois-Rivières, Quebec, Canada. Their son Jacques Bertault Jr. did not live to be an adult. He passed away in his home town at the age of twelve. Another child, Nicolas Bertault, died at the age of ten in 1672, in the same town.

"As was the custom, a marriage contract was brokered between their daughter Elisabeth Therese whom everyone called Isabelle, and Julien De LaTouche (1641–1772). Isabelle was twelve years old and Julien was thirty-one years old when they married on August 12, 1671. They were married in Trois-Rivières, Quebec, Canada.

"Early on, the marriage began to fracture in several places. To begin with, Julien De LaTouche quit his outside job to give full time-service to his own farm. Because he was lazy by nature, the ground was never plowed for the seeds to be planted, grown, and harvested. Because they did not grow their own food, the husband would send his wife to her parents' home to beg for food. Whenever he thought that Isabelle was too slow in making the round trip, he would beat her severely. The parents could not help but notice the welts, bruises, and black eyes on their precious daughter. Gillette and Jacques warned Julien several times about the beatings and his lack of work ethic. They got so tired of looking at their daughter, who was raggedy and pitiful. So, out of anguish, desperation, and fear for their daughter's safety, the parents plotted to kill Julien. It would have been no good to solicit help from the sheriff because there was no law against a husband beating his wife. With the collusion of Isabelle, Julien was invited to eat at his in-laws' house. They served him soup with poison leaves in it. Isabelle, acting as a dutiful wife, served him the soup with good conversation. Somehow, Julien did not reel over dead from the poison.

"The following day, the Bertaults went to Julien's farm with murder on their minds. Upon arriving, they went to the home and asked Isabelle, 'Where is your husband?'

"Isabelle replied, 'He is sitting in the barn drinking his liquor.'

"Then Gillette and Jacques went into the barn and they found, where Julien had been drinking during the early part of the day. His head was slumped down. They really thought he was either sleeping or in a drunken stupor. Gillette grabbed a shovel and hit him on the head.

"Up jumped Julien who screamed, 'What the hell!" Blood gushed out of his head, and he began to fight his in-laws. Oh, he was not as drunk as they thought!

"'Isabelle, Isabelle, come and help us!' they screamed.

"'Isabelle, Isabelle, come and help me!' Julien shouted.

"Isabelle ran to the barn and saw her husband battling her parents for his life while all the while blood was coming out of his head as he was screaming to the top of his lungs! Poor Isabelle was frozen in place. She did not know who to help. After her husband bled to death, from all the blows he received from the shovel and his father-in-law's fists, Isabelle was called to help drag her husband's lifeless body to the river. They dumped him in the bordering body of water. They thought no one would ever know who did it and they were hoping the body would never be found.

"Because they believed no one knew about what they did, Jacques, Gillette, and Isabelle went on with their lives as usual. However, the life and death screams of Julien had been overheard by people who were in an encampment in the surrounding woods. These people decided to go and tell the village sheriff about what they heard. They dared not go toward the direction of the screams because they did not want to take a chance in getting in harm's way. After hearing the story from the concerned people, the sheriff and two deputies immediately made their way to Julien De LaTouche's farm.

"It was two days later after the incident that the lawmen arrived at the farm. They knocked on the door of the farm house. Isabelle, who was alone, answered the door.

"'Madame De LaTouche, we have come to speak with your husband,' said the sheriff.

"'I am sorry sir, but my husband has gone hunting for food,' she replied anxiously.

"Now, this was a very suspicious answer because everyone in town knew that Julien De LaTouche was too lazy to hunt for food as well as he was too trifling to work for a living. He had been fired from all of his jobs for lack of performance. Nevertheless, not seeing anything suspicious, they left the home.

"Before they entered their wagons, the sheriff shouted, 'Let us check the barn for anything unusual.'

"Upon entering the barn, a sight was beheld! Nothing from the fight scene had been touched or cleaned. Blood was everywhere! One of Julien's shoes was found there. 'How can a man walking leave behind a shoe?' inquired one of the deputies.

"Even the bloody shovel was still lying in the straw on the floor of the barn. A decision was made to return to the farm house and to interrogate Julien's wife.

"'Madame, what do you have to say about the blood that is all over the barn?' asked the sheriff.

"'Oh, you mean where my husband killed an animal for food?' she answered.

"'Madame, you are double talking. How can your husband be out hunting for food when he has fresh kill from the fresh blood at his home?' drilled the sheriff.

"'Madame, how can a man go hunting and leave behind one of his only pair of work shoes?' ask one of the deputies.

"The young Isabelle soon buckled under the pressure of their intense questions. She made a confession of her part in the killing of her husband and she confessed about her parents' part also. She even brought the men to the spot in the water where the body had been dumped.

"In due time, Jacques Bertault, Gillette Marie Baune Banne, and Elisabeth Therese Isabelle Bertault appeared before the judge in the village court house. All of them were charged with murder. The sheriff and his deputies testified of the confession that Elisabeth made. Then the witnesses who first informed the sheriff told of the screams that they heard from Julien. His body was never found. Based on the testimonies, the three parties were found guilty of murder.

"Before their sentences were carried out, Jacques, Gillette, and Elisabeth had to kneel and crawl around the village square for people to throw rotten vegetables at them and to spit on them. Then they paused in front of the village church, where they prayed and were made to beg forgiveness from God, the king, and the Quebec government.

"Afterward, the government forced Gillette and Elisabeth to watch Jacques' execution by blows, bloodletting, and hanging. First his arms were crushed with hammers. In the same way, Jacques' thighs were broken. His blood came out of his body in a continuous stream. Then he was put on a wagon wheel for display in the village square. Finally, a rope was tied around his neck, and every time he moved or leaned forward or sideways, he slowly choked himself to death.

"On the same day, Gillette was hanged from the highest tree in the same public arena. Because of her age, Elisabeth was not executed. Nevertheless, all the property that Jacques, Gillette, and Elisabeth owned was confiscated and sold. All the proceeds were divided between the king of France and the Quebec government. The date of the execution was June 9, 1672, in Trois-Rivières, Quebec, Canada. Jacques Bertault was forty-six years old, and Gillette Marie Baune Banne was thirty-six years old. They had been married eighteen years.

"Meanwhile, Gillette's oldest child, Marie Chauvin, first married Robin Langlois (1637–1665) on November 25, 1664. She was fourteen years old and he was twenty-seven years old. Robin died one year after he was married. However, they had one child, whose name was Adrien Langlois (1665–1670). Adrien passed away at the age of five. After her husband's death, Marie Chauvin married for the second time to Jean Desnoyers (1635–1692) on July 20, 1665. They were married in Trois-Rivières, Quebec, Canada. This marriage produced nine children. The names of those children were Guillaume Desnoyers (1666–1704), Jacques Desnoyers (1668–1745), Marie Therese Desnoyers (1671–1750), Marguerite Desnoyers (1673–1724), Suzanne Desnoyers (1676–1681), Francois Desnoyers (1678–1778), Jean Baptiste Desnoyers (1686–1745), Louise Desnoyers (1690–1730), and St. Laurent Desnoyers (1691–1729).

"Their son, St. Laurent Desnoyers, chose to make his way to the Louisiana settlement of Natchez with the purpose of trying to find his fortune. There he met Angelique Chartra and decided to marry her. Angelique Chartra was born in Natchez on June 15, 1699. Her mother died while she was being born and her father died with a fever.

"St. Laurent and Angelique's daughter, Marie Louise Desnoyers, was born in the Natchez colony in 1723. Sometime after her birth, the couple sold their assets and bought land for a plantation in Ponte Coupee Parish. There she met Pierre Ricard, who had arrived from France in 1718. Again, they were married on January 7, 1745. Marie died before Pierre. She was fifty years old. He did not survive her very long. He died shortly during the same month of March as she did in 1773. People say he grieved himself to death by refusing to eat. He died at the age of seventy-one while he was sitting in a chair outside on his gallery."

CHAPTER 4

CREATING A MIND DISTURBANCE

"Miss Marie Claire, I can tell you are very proud of your family," said the young man. "Please, tell me why you are so proud of your lineage?"

"Sir, the one thing that separated our families, who owned plantations, from other free people of color was pedigree."

"What do you mean by colored people having pedigree?" the census taker inquired.

"Well, having pedigree meant that members of our families were hardly ever slaves; they could trace their African side straight back to their tribes, and they could trace their white side to France or Spain."

"Ma'am, I would like to ask you a question that you might find prying or very personal," said the census taker in a very low and thoughtful voice.

While he was talking, Miss Marie Claire was feeling very proud to be addressed as "ma'am" once again. No colored lady these days was ever addressed as "ma'am," and especially by a white gentleman. "Do, sir, go ahead and ask your question," she remarked.

"Well, Miss Marie Claire DeCuir, who was the first white

planter to marry or cohabit with a colored person in your family?" he hesitantly asked.

"Sir, that is a hard question to answer. That is why I didn't answer you yesterday. I did hear you. But, you see, the answer is perplexing. The reason why it is perplexing is that the white planters in my family married and cohabited with free women of color, and very seldom a slave, on so many levels of family kinships—for instance, grandparents, parents, uncles, brothers, cousins, and the like. Sometimes these alliances began around the same time. There were no telegraphs back then to send out social announcements."

"Can you provide me with any intimate details on these relationships?"

"You know, sir, at the age of one hundred and five, I cannot remember everything in chronological order. The best thing I can do is relate to you the incidents and small stories of the lives of family guests that attended my daughter's wedding in 1831. My daughter fwc Cydalise Celenie Porche, the mother of my grandson fmc Louis Ricard, was the bride. Her wedding was such a grand and fabulous affair the likes of which has not been seen since. Most of the relatives who were alive and healthy came, both white and colored."

"My, that sounds intriguing," he said. "Do go on with the story!"

"There was no better day than a sunny day of February 15, 1831, to get married in Pointe Coupee Parish. On this date, my daughter, fwc Cydalise Celenie Porche, (1816–1862), married fmc Pierre St. Luc Ricard IV, (1805–1886). The beaming couple said their vows on the veranda of the house as the parents and guests stood on the grounds of the Porche's plantation.

"My family, the DeCuirs and Porches, was so overjoyed that Cydalise was marrying into the Ricard family. It was almost like marrying into a royal family! The Porche and DeCuir families, of course, had money, but no free family had as much money in the world as the Ricard family. They had plantations in Pointe Coupee and Iberville Parishes. All the Ricard siblings and their children had grand plantation mansions.

"It was the best of times for Cydalise and Pierre St. Luc IV to marry. This elaborate wedding occurred during the Antebellum Period of the South. You seem to be too young to have been around during that period of history, but if you know your Louisiana and Southern history from school, the Antebellum Period was the most glorious period of the South. There was and probably will be no other grander period than that time. That was a time when there was plenty crop growth and markets to sell them. There were no droughts. The slaves worked very hard, and they were very happy! How do I know the slaves were happy? They sang their tunes all the while they worked. Now, I ask you, would you sing while you worked and you were not happy? Everyone benefited from this time.

"Little did we know how drastically things would change as the talk of war actually became war. Because the families of the groom and my family were wealthy planters and slave owners, they benefited economically at this time because cotton was king! Tobacco, indigo, and rice were not doing badly, either. Why, they could not export enough cotton to the North and to foreign countries!

"So only your imagination could picture how the wedding guests appeared on the plantation grounds as the couple exchanged their vows in front of a priest. All of the Ricards and their extended family were present. Each of them—brothers, sisters, mothers, fathers, cousins, in-laws, and out-laws (black sheep)—were known by name by me. It's not that I was a nosy woman; I just knew stuff. Why, I knew the beginnings, the intimate stories, the scandals, and the gossip of all these important colored and white folk who were somehow related to the Ricards.

"Because no air was moving and everyone could not fit under the shade of the sycamore tree, there was a lot of agitation going on. I saw that each of the madams and mademoiselles were suffering because they were being parched by the sun and I could do nothing about it. Each female had her personal slave lady fan her with a very small palmetto tree branch.

"And then they all, both men and women, had either a slave man or a slave lady waiting next to them holding small decorated drawstring bags. I knew exactly the purposes of these bags. All the bags held folded white cotton strips of assorted sizes. When men and ladies had to go inside the mansion to use or sit on the slop jar, their slave would hand them cotton strips to wipe themselves. The used cotton strips would be handed to the slave, who would then fold them and place them in the drawstring purse.

"If a lady was on her monthly and needed to change, she would go inside the mansion with her slave girl and the girl would reach her a clean cotton strip. In exchange the slave would deposit the dirty one in the drawstring bag.

"Each baby and small child ten and under had a personal slave who either held or followed them for the duration of the wedding to take care of their personal needs, such as wet nursing, feeding, changing diapers, and taking them to relieve themselves. All dirty cotton strip diapers were placed inside the drawstring bag, no matter how they got dirty.

"When the slaves who held those bags, returned to their own plantation home, they had to be responsible for shaking the mess in the woods. Then they had the hard chores of boiling, bleaching, cleaning, and hanging the cotton cloths on the clothes line for another day's use.

"My, oh my, it was a hot and humid day for both the families of my daughter, Cydalise Celenie Porche and of the groom, Pierre St. Luc Ricard IV. The families were dutifully present to witness the nuptials. These free persons of color, their white relatives, and the slaves all perspired together in the heat. Some of them had travelled very far. Why, some folk came from as far away as the big city of New Orleans!

"They all came with their personal small riding wagons with high stepping beautiful stallions. All of them had their slaves drive covered wagons for sleep accommodations of the family. Some had not seen each other for a long time. Somehow, they quickly caught up on the excitement of new births, new marriages, new engagements, and recent deaths. Unfortunately, to my memory, this was the last very large occasion where our white and colored relatives would be together as equals and acknowledged their relationship. There was a very dark cloud brewing overhead, but you could not see it with the naked eye. You needed the assistance of a tea reader, a card reader, or some sort of fortune teller to inform you of the cruelties of war, financial disasters, and separations of families that were ahead of us.

"The mother of the groom, fwc Marguerite Marie Antoinette Belly (1786–1846), was present. But unfortunately, his father, fmc Pierre St. Luc Ricard (1758–1814), was deceased. The groom's brother and best man, fmc Antoine St. Luc Ricard (1813–1873), was there with his wife, fwc Marie Leda Tounoir (1816–1872) of Pointe Coupee Parish. Antoine St. Luc Ricard was born the year (1813) before his father died. He never knew him.

"The groom's aunt, fwc Rosalie Belly (1785–1850), the widow of fmc Antoine Dubuclet Sr. (1773–1828), was there with her twelve children and their spouses. Now, the father of fmc Antoine Dubuclet Sr., was Josephe Antoine DuBuclet D'Hauterive (1744–), who emigrated from Hauterive, France. He was given a land grant from France to settle in Louisiana. This land grant was large enough for an immense plantation. He married fwc Marie Felicite Gray of Louisiana in the eighteenth century. They had a hard life in the beginning because all the trees had to be cut down for planting crops. The wood from the trees made a handsome looking mansion. The left over trees were used to build a barn and to build shelters for slaves.

"Since all twelve of the groom's Dubuclet cousins were alive for the wedding, they came as follows: fwc Marie Felicite Dubuclet (1802–)

was escorted by her husband, Francois Fortin of Iberville Parish; fwc Rosalie Petronille Dubuclet (1805–1850) was escorted by her husband, fmc Jean Baptiste Hubeau (1799–1839) of East Baton Rouge Parish; fwc Marie Solitaire Dubuclet (1807–); fmc Zacharie Honore Dubuclet (1810–); fmc Antoine Dubuclet Jr. (1810–1887) escorted his wife, fwc Claire Pollard (1809–1851); fmc Francois Uranie Dubuclet (1811); fwc Marie Petronille Dubuclet (1815–); fwc Josephine Delphine Dubuclet (1816–) was escorted by her fiancé, fmc Antoine DeCuir, Jr. (1816–1865) of Pointe Coupee Parish; fwc Hortense Dubuclet (1817–); fmc Augustin Dubuclet (1819–1889); fmc George Dubuclet (1822–); and fmc Honorine Evelina Dubuclet (1824–).

"Now, fwc Rosalie Petronille Dubuclet married fmc Jean Baptiste Hubeau on April 10, 1820, in St. Gabriel, Iberville, Parish. Jean Baptiste was the son of the plantation owners Paul Hubeau (1756–1822) and fwc Marie Devin, both of East Baton Rouge Parish. Rosalie and Jean Baptiste came with their children, who were fwc Rose Hubeau (1821–), fmc Paul Duplain Hubeau (1823–), fwc Felicite Eulodie Hubeau (1827–), and fmc L. Hubeau (1828–).

"My niece, fwc Claire Pollard, was married to fmc Antoine Dubuclet Jr. Claire was the second child of my whole sister, fwc Eugenie DeCuir (1790–1839) and her husband, Louis Pollard II (1770–1824). Claire and Antoine Dubuclet Jr. had been married in Iberville Parish in 1830. After they were married, they moved to the Pollard Plantation in Pointe Coupee Parish. The owner of the Pollard Plantation was Louis Pollard II, who had been born in St. Hilaire en Lez, Bretagne, France, and he died in Lakeland, Pointe Coupee Parish in 1824, in his home. His French parents were Louis Pollard I (1745–) and Marie Fanne du Barsconet (1745–), and both of them lived all their lives in St. Hilaire en Lez, Bretagne, France.

"As for fwc Josephine Delphine Dubuclet, her fiancé, fmc Antoine DeCuir Jr., Pointe Coupee Parish, was the son of my brother, fmc

Antoine DeCuir Sr. (1788–1843), which made him my nephew. My brother, Antoine married Antoine Jr.'s, mother in 1810 in Pointe Coupee Parish. Her name was fwc Pouponne DeCoux (1786–1836). Pouponne was the daughter of Jean Pierre DeCoux (1743–1797) and fwc Modeste Balquet.

"I can tell you that fmc Antoine DeCuir Jr. was twice related to me because his mother, fwc Pouponne DeCoux's father, Jean Pierre DeCoux (1743–1797) of Pointe Coupee Parish, was the son of Jacques DeCoux (1692–1756) of Namur, Haimut, Belgium and Anne Catherine DeCuir (1703–1775). Anne Catherine DeCuir was the whole sister to my grandfather, Jean Pierre Francois DeCuir (1704–1771). This Jean Pierre Francois DeCuir and his wife, Genevieve Mayeux (1727–1779), were the parents of my father Joseph Antoine DeCuir. You see now?

"Let me elaborate more about my brother fmc Antoine DeCuir Sr. My brother Antoine had a penchant for loving three women at the same time. When it came to providing for them, cost was no object! He spared no cost for the lavish lifestyle he provided for his two wives and his lady fwc Sophie Deslonde (1779–1836) and their children. He made sure that all of them had palatial accommodations in sumptuous mansions that were designed by the best architects of that time. Even though the ladies had luxurious accommodations, the homes were not at all equal in appearance, size, and amenities. If I had to say which residence was superior in all aspects, I would say that it was Riverlake, which he built for his future bride, fwc Louise Suisienne Beauvais (1786–1871), whom he married in 1823. She was the wealthy widow of the late planter Charles Adolphe Tanneret (1790–1820). Therefore, my brother had to really display his feelings for her to beat the competition. She had a lot of suitors even in her thirties with children, because she was already rich. Antoine separated himself from the pack by building a house like Riverlake for her.

"Each woman and child on his plantation had slaves to attend to his every need and to plant private gardens so that fresh vegetables and fruits could always be available. It was very complicated for him to spend equal time with each female and to make sure that his time with one of them did not overlap time that was supposed to be for another one. How he managed to juggle both time and space remains a mystery to me. With the kind of funds my brother had during this bustling economic period, he could easily make the women happy in their provisions. Even at his death in 1843, my brother, Antoine, was noted in the newspaper obituary as being one of the wealthiest men in the whole United States of America.

"In the name of family peace and for me to not to show favoritism, Antoine's wives, fwc Pouponne DeCoux and fwc Louise Suisienne Beauvais, and his lady, fwc Sophie Deslonde, were invited to the wedding. Louise brought all her children to the wedding. They were fmc Adolphe Tanneret (1811–1886), fmc Emile Tanneret (1815–), and fwc Antoinette DeCuir (1826–). Antoinette would be the only child that my brother would father with Louise.

"Antoine's lady, fwc Sophie Deslonde at the time of my daughter's wedding lived in her own mansion on the far side of Antoine's plantation. Her living circumstances finally got to her, and she had begun showing signs of fatigue and mental anguish because Antoine never asked her to marry him. Often he tried in several ways to spark romantic notions in her. She somehow managed to keep refusing his desires for more intimacy. At the beginning of their relationship, she had been true, loving, and affectionate to him. She felt emotionally neglected because he married twice on her. So she took their children to the house he built for her, and she vowed never to be intimate with him again. Her living children, whom she brought to the wedding, were fmc Therance DeCuir (1790–1837), fmc Leandre DeCuir (1799–1838), fwc Adeline DeCuir (1800–1859), fmc Remy DeCuir (1802–1866), fmc Dorsin DeCuir

(1806–1884), fwc Delphine DeCuir (1811–1869), and fmc Armand DeCuir (1816–1865).

"A second aunt of the groom in attendance was fwc Marie Genevieve Belly (1789–), who was the widow of fmc Cyprien Ricard (1783–1826). Marie Genevieve and Cyprien were married in 1806 in the town of St. Gabriel, Iberville Parish. This couple spent the rest of their married lives in Iberville Parish on their vast plantation holdings. Don't forget that this renowned Cyprien Ricard had more wealth than any free person of color in the whole country during his time. Of course, her children accompanied her to the wedding. They were fmc Pierre Cyprien Ricard (1808–), fmc Lucien Ricard (1819–), fmc Joseph Ricard (1825–), fwc Delphine Antoinette Ricard (1813–1834), fwc Basilide Ricard (1814–1842), and fmc Maximilian Octave Ricard (1809–1845). Maximilian's wife, fwc Marie Louise Portales, and their daughter, fwc Louise Ricard (1823–1850), were there too.

"A guest of fmc Pierre Cyprien Ricard was his fiancée, fwc Marie Rose Catiche Honore Destrehan (1814–1859), of Iberville Parish. As was the custom, both Marie Rose's parents were present as chaperones. The parents' names were fmc Jean Francois Honore Destrehan Sr. (1789–1842) and fwc Marie Celeste DeCuir (1795–1842). Marie Celeste DeCuir was my whole sister because we had the same parents.

"My sister's husband was a descendent of the Honore Destrehan Family, which had many plantations and an abundance of slaves in Iberville Parish, St. John the Baptist Parish, St. Charles Parish, and Jefferson Parish. My sister and her husband were married in 1810 in Iberville Parish. His parents were the wealthy Jean Baptiste Honore Destrehan (1772–1802) and fwc Marie Felicite Gue Gravier (1772–). Jean Baptiste Honore Destrehan was the first of his family to marry someone of African descent. Marie Felicite had been born in Guinea, Africa. They lived together on the plantation and raised a lovely family. They were married in 1789, which was three years before he died. Everyone knows how hard it was for him to finally commit to marriage. Before his relationship with Marie Felicite, he had a prior intimate relationship on his plantation that lasted several years. That lady's name was fwc Genevieve Iris Bienville, of Iberville Parish. She was a freed slave of the explorer and the governor, Bienville. They had one child, fwc Catherine Honore Destrehan (1749–1794). Catherine Honore Destrehan married her uncle, whose name was Pompe Honore Destrehan (1745–). Catherine's father and her husband had the same parents. Pompe Honore Destrehan was the second member of his family, who married someone of African descent.

"Please, I must digress and say something about that Honore Destrehan family. It's nothing nice, but it is the truth. Remember, I just told you how the Honore Destrehan Family became mixed with free people of Color. The members of the Honore Destrehan Family, whether white or colored, in Louisiana, have the same great-grandparents, which makes them all of the same and kin, you see?

"The parents of the brothers Jean Baptiste Honore Destrehan and Pompe Honore Destrehan were Jean Baptiste Honore Destrehan de Beaupre (1700–1765) and Jeanne Catherine de Gauvery (1718–1762). Their father was born in Tours, Indre-et-Loire, Centre, France. While their mother was born in Tours, Pay-de-Dome, Auvergne, France. Both parents arrived in New Orleans in 1722. The French government had appointed Jean Baptiste as treasurer of the Marine and comptroller for the Louisiana Colony. Jean Baptiste Honore Destrehan and his wife, Jeanne Catherine de Gauvery, were awarded vast acres of land on the East Bank and West Bank of the Mississippi River as a reward for their faithful service. This land grant crossed several of today's parish boundaries. They raised enough children so that all their land would be family controlled when their children were grown and had their own families. The family, of course, was very, very wealthy. These were the names of their other children: Charles Honore Destrehan (1745–), Jeanne

Marguerite Marie Honore Destrehan (1751–1814), Jeanne Catherine Honore Destrehan (1753–1773), Marie Elizabeth Honore Destrehan (1755–1817), Marie Elizabeth Isabel Honore Destrehan (1755–1779), Jean Baptiste Louis Honore Destrehan (1758–1776), Jean Noel Honore Destrehan (1759–1823), and Jean Francois Honore Destrehan (–1842).

"Sometimes during this century, there was a nasty contention of the white family members over the use of the Honore Destrehan name by the colored people of the family. The white people of the family gradually began to disassociate themselves from the free colored people of the family. The fight was not about land or money because all of them were rich. The family branch of the white people generally didn't want the colored branch to marry their family members, and they didn't want them to use their name. I tell you, it was horrible the way the free people of color were misused!

"This is what I mean. I heard that big money was passed to government officials and to priests. Why, you might ask? The plan that the white folks came up with was to divide the name. The civil officials and the religious authorities were bribed to register all colored births, baptisms, weddings, and deaths with the surname of Honore. As for the white people in the family, they would be registered as Destrehan. Are there any white people with the name Honore? Yes, because after the Civil War, times got rough, and people went as far as New Orleans and further to pass for white if they could. Are there any colored people with the name Destrehan? Yes, because every now and then a dark-skinned colored baby is born in a white family named Destrehan. There are just some things that you cannot run from, you see?

"I hope I did not bore you with that little tidbit of information—which is more than gossip; it's the truth! Now, as for my daughter's wedding, fmc Jean Francois Honore Destrehan and my whole, sister fwc Marie Celeste DeCuir, brought their other children to the wedding. They were the twins fwc Jeanne Francoise Honore Destrehan (1811–)

and fmc Jean Francois Honore Destrehan Jr. (1811–1890), fmc Zacherie Honore Destrehan (1814–), fwc Eugenie Honore Destrehan (1818–), fwc Marie Celeste Honore Destrehan (1823–1859), and fwc Marie Antoinette Adeline Honore Destrehan (1824–).

"The third aunt of the groom who arrived was fwc Valerie Octavine Belly (1790–1880) and her husband, fmc Paulin Verret (1796–1836). Iberville Parish was the home of the Verret's auspicious mansion and plantation. Their living children accompanied them and their names were fmc Paulin Alcee Verret (1819–), fmc Nicolas Verret (1823–), fmc Guillaume Belly Verret (1828–), fmc Jules Verret (1830–), fwc Valerie Octavine Verret (1821–), and fwc Rose Marie Anne Verret (1825–).

"A fourth aunt at the wedding was fwc Clothilde Valerie Belly (1790–1833) and her husband, Auguste Borie Solomon of Iberville Parish. The fifth aunt of the groom who arrived was fwc Marie Francoise Belly (1800–1872). At the time of the wedding, she was already thirty-one years old. Poor sweetie, she had never had a beau. Everyone thought she was doomed to be a spinster. She came unescorted to the wedding.

"Another aunt at the wedding was fwc Heloise Marguerite Belly (1808–1880) and her spouse, fmc George Deslondes Jr. (1808–1889). Her husband was from St. Charles Parish. The Deslondes family had been living in the formally named German Coast since the eighteenth century because the French government gave his grandparents, Pierre Jean Baptiste Deslondes (1714–1761) and Anna Barbe Paume (1718–1753) of Normandie, France, a generous land grant. George Deslondes Jr.'s parents were George Deslondes Sr. (1754–) and fwc Felicite Brule (1780–1858). The marriage of fmc George Deslondes Jr. and fwc Heloise Marguerite Belly occurred in 1822 in St. Gabriel, Iberville Parish. To my daughter's wedding, they brought their children fwc Marie Felicite Odile Deslondes (1823–) and fmc Pierre George Deslondes (1825–1885).

"The sisters of the groom's father, fmc Pierre St. Luc Ricard, were there. The first sister was fwc Adelaide Ricard (1769–1850), who was the widow of fmc Antoine Henri Colin LaCour (1767–1818) of Pointe Coupee Parish. Adelaide was accompanied by her children who were fwc Francoise Colin LaCour (–1832), fwc Genevieve Colin LaCour, fwc Marie Marthe Colin LaCour, fwc Celestine Colin LaCour (1787–), fmc Sosthene Agicole Colin LaCour (1792–1862), fmc Cyprien Colin LaCour (1813–1889), fmc Gervais Colin LaCour (1810–1850), and fmc Rosemond Colin LaCour (1818–1850).

"Their son, fmc Gervais Colin LaCour, was there with his wife, fwc Augustine Robert (1805–1855) and their son, baby fmc Henri LaCour (1831–1860). Augustine Robert was from Pointe Coupee Parish. Also, Adelaide's son, fmc Rosemond LaCour, was there with his spouse, fwc Adele Desrosiers (–1886), of Pointe Coupee Parish, and their children, fwc Adele LaCour (1826–), fwc Amelida LaCour (1828–), and fwc Claire LaCour (1830–).

"Three siblings of the groom's father attended the wedding unescorted. Their names were fwc Hortense De Rieutard Ricard (1815–1853), fwc Claire Ricard, and fmc Agicole Ricard. At the time of the wedding, they were not married. To think of it, I don't remember if they ever got married and had children.

"One uncle of the groom, fmc Maximilian Ricard (1786–1823), and his wife, fwc Marie Louise Portateie (–1829), were deceased. However, their children represented their family at the wedding. Representing their parents were fwc Clothilde Ricard (1813–), fwc Telcide Ricard (1817–1836), fmc Paulin Ricard (1820–), and fwc Marie Louise Ricard (1824–). Their legal guardians and their personal slaves accompanied them.

"Representing another sibling of the groom's grandfather, the late Antoine DeRieutard Ricard, was the surviving child of Antoine's sister. His sister was the late Marie Louise Ricard (1745–1814). Marie Louise's husband was the deceased Jean Francois Allain III (1739–1805). Marie

Louise's surviving child was Hyacinthe Allain (1784–1874). She was attending the wedding with her children and her husband Charles Morgan, Sr. (1775–1848). Charles Morgan was peculiar at this wedding because he was the only American in attendance. People whispered about him because the Americans were usually not invited to the social events of the Creoles."

"'Look! His clothes are so plain and ugly,' I heard one relative say.

"Americans were considered loud, unbathed, smelly, and ignorant of the social graces. He was from New Jersey. When he immigrated to Louisiana, he broke the laws of New Jersey by bringing his slaves with him to what he called the Morganza Plantation in Pointe Coupee Parish. He eventually became the first American sheriff of Pointe Coupee Parish. The town of Morganza in Pointe Coupee Parish is named for him. How astonished Charles Morgan must have been at what he observed at the wedding! He had not been raised to socialize with colored people. He did not understand the reasons why the colored people acted and talked to him as though they were his equals."

"'Who are these colored people, and why are they standing around talking to white people?' I heard him say to his wife.

"She whispered, 'These colored people and white people are related to each other, and they are related to me.'

"Why, he did not know of any free persons of color in New Jersey who owned slaves! The children of Hyacinthe Allain and Charles Morgan were Marie Francoise Morgan (1808–), Adeline Allain Morgan (1810–1839), Augustine Morgan (1813–), Charles Morgan Jr. (1815–1860), Roltus Morgan (1818–), James Alfred Morgan (1820–1890), A. J. Morgan (1823–1890), and Aurora Marguerite Morgan (1812–). With Marguerite was her husband William Ramsey Falconer, MD. (1810–1841). These two were married in 1828 in Pointe Coupee Parish. They brought their baby, Charles Augustus Falconer (1831–1862), with them to the wedding."

CHAPTER 5

GENTEEL LADIES, GALLANT GENTLEMEN

"Whoa! That was a grand amount of people you had attending your daughter's wedding. You were correct in that they were mixed on so many different levels of relationships. What about your family? Were they able to attend? Did they bring their Colored spouses and mixed breed children?" inquired the census taker.

"Well, sir, I felt so sorrowful that my husband, fmc Raymond Porche, could not join me as I watched our daughter, Cydalise Celenie, on her most joyous day. My husband and I were married on January 5, 1815, in Pointe Coupee Parish. We raised our family on the same Porche Plantation. From our marriage came our blessed children, fwc Marie Aspasie Porche (1814–1862), fmc Leonard Porche (1820–), fmc Hypolite Porche (1825–1910), and of course, the bride, fwc Cydalise Celenie Porche (1816–1862).

"Well, I have explained to you how those other families became mixed, and now I will tell you how the same thing happened to the Porche Family. Raymond Porche's father was Hypolite Porche (1769–1820). Hypolite was born and raised on his family's plantation in Pointe

Coupee Parish. He died there. Raymond's mother, fwc Francoise Franchonette DeCuir (1777–1844), was born in Pointe Coupee on her family's plantation and died in New Orleans.

"Hypolite's father was Vincent I. Alexis Le Porche (1709–1775) of Vannes, Morbihan, Bretagne, France. Vincent's wife was Marie Francois Pauque Poche (1729–1802). She was one of a few white ladies born in colonial Louisiana. In 1720, Vincent, at age eleven, emigrated from France along with his parents Jacques Le Porche (1675–1731) and Philiberte Quinton, (1675–1745) and his siblings, Marie Anne Le Porche (1689–), Pierre Augustin Le Porche (1699–1777), Hypolite Le Porche (1712–), Francois Le Porche (1714–), Jan Le Porche (1690–), and Francoise Le Porche (1695–1730) The father, Jacques, and his mother, Philiberte, were born in Vannes, Morbihan, Bretagne, France. The father of Jacque Le Porche was Jan Le Porche, who was born in 1653 and died in 1733. There exists no record for Jan's wife. Jan Le Porche was born in Pestivien, Cotes Bretagne, France. He died there too.

"The parents of Vincent I. Alexis Le Porche's parents were able to obtain a large government land grant to settle in the outlying land of Pointe Coupee. They built a large plantation. They were delighted living with their children and grandchildren. Crops were bountiful, and their slaves sang joyfully all the time. Eventually, these parents died of natural causes in Pointe Coupee Parish.

"The strikingly beautiful Marie Francoise Pauque Poche (1729–1802) caught Vincent I. Alexis Le Porche's eyes. After an appropriate courtship, a marriage contract was arranged. They were able to marry on November 23, 1745, at St. Francis Catholic Church in Pointe Coupee Parish. Vincent was thirty-six years old at the time and Marie Francoise was only fifteen years old. Vincent and his wife lived on his large, thriving plantation, which grew a variety of crops suitable for the climate and the time of year. Their plantation was located adjacent to those of Vincent's brothers, Pierre and Hypolite, near False River in Pointe Coupee Parish. They prospered with the free labor force of many slaves. Both Vincent and Marie Francoise died in Pointe Coupee Parish. Vincent died in 1775, while his wife died in 1802. Vincent and Marie Francoise had eleven children in their marriage. Their names were Pierre Joseph Porche (1748–1810), Marie Augustine Porche (1750–1807), Marie Anna Porche (1753–1793), Jean Francois Porche (1756–1820), Simon Porche (1758–1859), Joseph Porche (1760–), Vincent Alexis Porche (1761–1830), Alexis Porche (1764–), Genevieve Porche (1766–), Hypolite Porche (1769–1820), Joachim Porche (1779–1809), and Jean Baptiste Porche (1780–).

"Vincent I. Alexis Le Porche did have another child with another woman. The name of the child was fwc Marie Louise Porche (1746–1802). Her mother was a slave. As was the custom of the Creole planters in rural Louisiana, Vincent freed his daughter, gave her his surname, and made her a legal heir to his property. She lived very well while her father was alive and after he was dead.

"The surviving children of Vincent I. Alexis Le Porche were invited to the wedding. Simon Porche and Genevieve Porche were the surviving children of Vincent who were there. Having no spouses, they went to the wedding together.

"Attending this large family wedding were the surviving children of Vincent's late son, Pierre Joseph Porche, and his deceased wife, Brigitte Guerin (1769–1810). Their daughter, Augustine Porche (1799–), and her spouse, Carlos Poree (1790–), were in attendance. Julie Porche (1800–) and her brother, Etienne Porche (1802–), attended together.

"Their sister, Helene Porche (1800–1842), and her husband, Severin Porche (1798–1840), were there. It seemed Helene and Severin had received a dispensation to marry each other from a Catholic priest. This was arranged so they could keep the family's money and property in the family. They were first cousins who were the grandchildren of Vincent I. Alexis Le Porche and Marie Francoise Pauque Poche. Severin's parents were Vincent's son, Jean Francois Porche, and Perrine Petronilla Barras (1764–1840). Helene's parents were Vincent's son, Pierre Joseph Porche, and Brigitte Guerin. Helene's brother, Pierre Joseph Porche Jr. (1804–1876), and his wife, Celine Gremillion (1810–1838) were wedding guests along with their two-year-old child, Josephine Porche (1829–1888).

"Also invited was the family of Vincent I. Alexis Le Porche's deceased daughter, fwc Marie Louise Porche, and her husband, Jean Baptiste Dugue-Reuter Sr. (1740–1778). They were married in 1761 in Pointe Coupee Parish. Huh, I must remind you that the mother of Marie Louise was an unnamed slave and not a free woman of color.

"One daughter of Marie Louise was fwc Marie Josephe Dugue-Reuter (1762–), the wealthy widow of Joseph Daigle whom she married in 1782 and the rich widow of Jacques Bebe whom she married in 1794. She arrived with her siblings, fmc Jean Baptiste Dugue-Reuter (1768–) and fmc Francois Dugue-Reuter (1773–). They were fwc Marie Louise Porche's children with her first husband, the late and wealthy planter Jean Baptiste Dugue-Reuter (1740–1778).

"After Marie Louise Porche's husband died suddenly in 1778, she immediately married the late Elias Lafitte (1750–1802), a wealthy plantation owner in Pointe Coupee Parish. Soon after, in the same year, Marie Louise's youngest daughter, fwc Charlotte Lafitte (1778–1840), was born. Charlotte arrived to the wedding with her husband, Louis Ambroise LaCour Sr. (1769–), and their children, fwc Philomene LaCour, fwc Charlotte Marie LaCour (1813–1864), and fwc Marguerite LaCour (1816–1861).

"Of course there were more descendants of Vincent I. Alexis Le Porche of both races present at the wedding. It was not amazing that they all knew each other. The rural areas of Louisiana were similar to other small towns. The rich people seemed to get along very well. They were also blood relatives, and they respected each other's position in the family. Since they were all very wealthy, there were no petty jealousies over how much money they possessed. During the Colonial and the Antebellum periods of Louisiana, especially in the rural parishes, there were hardly any clashes along racial lines with the plantation owners. They were primarily concerned with increasing their wealth by increasing the production of their crops, increasing their slave workforce, and having their children marry up in the social and economic scale.

"Other Porche family at the wedding was Evariste Porche (–1865) and his spouse Julie Lejeune. With them was their daughter, two-year-old Ladoiska Porche (1829–). Elvire Porche (–1889) was accompanied by her fiancé, Eugene Chassaignac (–1880). Elvire and Eugene were married in 1842. Evariste and Elvire were the children of Helene Porche and Severin Porche Sr. Helene and Severin brought along their unmarried children Marie Helene Porche (1823–1847), Francois Porche (1827–1865), and Severin Porche Jr. (1821–) Even at their early ages, Francois Porche, age four, and his niece Ladoiska Porche, age two, had a signed marriage contract that they would fulfill on January 1, 1848, in Pointe Coupee Parish. They were able to have that contract as uncle and niece to marry each other and keep the wealth in the family because Helene Porche and Severin Porche, Jr. had obtained a dispensation from a Catholic priest for that purpose.

"Other members of the Porche family present were the families of the late fwc Genevieve Dugue-Reuter (1770–1817) and her late husband, Julien Etienne Broyard Barre (1756–1817). Fwc Genevieve Dugue-Reuter was the daughter of fwc Marie Louise Porche and Jean Baptiste Dugue-Reuter. The marriage of fwc Genevieve Dugue-Reuter and Julien Etienne Broyard Barre occurred on February 6, 1790, in Pointe Coupee Parish. Their daughter, fwc Constance Broyard Barre (1804–), and her husband, Hypolite Guillot (1789–), were also guests. They had been married in Pointe Coupee Parish on January 13, 1824.

A son, fmc Evariste Broyard Barre (1808–1849), came with his wife, fwc Marceline Gaspard.

"Another daughter, fwc Rosalie (Rosalind) Broyard Barre, called 'the dark one' because of her midnight hue complexion, came with her husband Antoine Mayeux (1798–1842), whom she had married on June 24, 1817, in Pointe Coupee Parish. They brought their son, fmc Palmire Mayeux (1825–), and daughter, fwc Scholastique Mayeux (1829–), with them. Their two other daughters were allowed to bring their fiancés to the wedding. So then, eleven-year-old fwc Antoinette Mayeux (1820–1880) was escorted by eleven-year-old Faustin Bordelon (1820–1882). Antoinette and Faustin were married in Pointe Coupee Parish in 1837. Antoinette's twelve-year-old sister, fwc Emelie Mayeux (1819–1855), was escorted by seventeen-year-old Sosthene Alexander Couvillon (1814–1854). Emelie and Sosthene were married later on December 13, 1833, in Avoyelles Parish.

"Because Sosthene Alexander Couvillon of Hydropolis, Avoyelles Parish, was of the age of majority and both of his parents, Pierre Couvillon (1723–1825) and Bridgett Julia Mayeux (1785–1828), were dead, he was not required to have adult supervision. Besides, by the time of the wedding, his parents' succession had been done and he had inherited his part of their vast holdings.

"As for Faustin Bordelon, he was brought to the wedding by his parents and all his siblings came too. My, oh, my! What a loud and rowdy bunch! I still can't decide if they behaved the way that they did because they lived so far north of civilization in New Orleans in Bordelonville, Avoyelles Parish or was it because it was so many of them and they were very close in age. It was very puzzling to see white people with money act so wild. They were actually acting like those uncouth Americans who came to Louisiana after the Louisiana Purchase and those carpetbaggers that invaded the state after the Civil War. Well, anyway, Faustin's parents were Augustin Bordelon (1792–1860) and

Celeste Guillot (1798–1866). Their other children were Zenon Bordelon (1806–1852), Victoria Bordelon (1808–1849), Marguerite Bordelon (1816–1838), Augustin Gregoire Bordelon (1820–1880), Jean Pierre Bordelon (1821–1863), Jean Baptiste Bordelon (1823–1864), Celestine Bordelon (1825–), Doralise Bordelon (1827–1875), Epesipe Vege Bordelon (1828–1854), and the twins, Azeline Bordelon (1829–) and Azema Bordelon (1829–1868). All these Bordelon people came to the wedding! They were very colorful, and the other guests were amused by their antics, clothes and the way they ate with their hands.

"Now on the other hand and in contrast to that Bordelon family, my family was always considered very classy and respectable. People admired the DeCuir family very much because they could trace their ancestors to fifteenth century Europe. We had abundant wealth also. It seemed many of the descendants of the children of Albert DeCuir (1673–1750) and Marie Catherine Jeanne Domer (1673–1738) became very successful as plantation owners.

"Their son, Jean Pierre Francois DeCuir, my grandfather, also had a son by a slave. His name was fmc Louis DeCuir (1772–1832). As was the custom in the frontier parts of the Louisiana colony, Louis was baptized with his father's surname. He was freed and given the same rights, education, status and heredity of his siblings. All of us knew Louis and we respected him and embraced him as our dearest of kin as brother and uncle. This did not happen to the children born of the masters in the American colonies.

"My late father, Joseph Antoine DeCuir, had two surviving brothers at the time of my daughter's wedding, and they came as honored guests of the wedding. Their names were fmc Louis DeCuir and Jean Baptiste Dorsin DeCuir. There was no wife or children for fmc Louis DeCuir at this time. However, Jean Baptiste Dorsin DeCuir brought his spouse, Helene Bourgeat (1775–) and their children Therence DeCuir (–1846), Jean Baptiste Dorsin DeCuir Jr. (1803–1849), and Martin DeCuir (1810–).

"An old man, now in his fifties, gray-haired and stooped from the waist, yet my uncle, fmc Louis DeCuir managed, with a lot of pain to come to the wedding. My Uncle Louis was well respected and admired for his dignity, wisdom, and quiet and thoughtful way of life. It was nothing about the cultured tone of my uncle's life that would have indicated his mother had been my grandfather's slave. His mother, Marguerite, was the slave. Marguerite had been born in Senegal of the Wolof tribe. She spoke only French. Uncle Louis had been a lifelong bachelor, and he never had any children. Louis had received his portion of my grandfather's estate. His share included land, slaves, livestock, and money. Unfortunately, the year following the wedding, my Uncle Louis died peacefully in his sleep at the old age of sixty.

"The widowed sister of my father was an honored guest. She was Marie Magdeleine DeCuir, the widow of Charles Alexander Barre (1746–1829), who was the owner of a huge plantation in Opelousas, St. Landry Parish. The couple married in Opelousas on April 9, 1771. The names of the children who accompanied their mother to the ceremony were Emelie Amilia Barre (1776–1853), Marie Genevieve Barre (1778–1843), Elena Barre (1781–1852), Euphrosine Barre (1788–1859), and Marie Louise Barre (1790–1843). I must inform you that Port Barre in St. Landry Parish was named for the Barre family.

"Emelie Amilia Barre was the widow of William Pitt Higbee (1770–1813). The two of them had been married in St. Martin Parish in 1811. Unfortunately, he didn't live long afterward. But on September 2, 1829, she married Joseph Bonaparte Gradenigo (1770–1833) in St. Landry Parish. She was escorted to the wedding by her second husband. Although the two of them were happy most of the time, the times she miscarried were the saddest of times for the both of them. Joseph never would allow himself to be anxious or anguished around his wife, Emelie Amilia. In private, he was truly troubled by not having direct heirs from his wife for his vast plantation estates, which included an enormous amount of slave workers to maintain his hundreds of acres. Twice before his marriage, he had established relationships with two other women, one a slave and one a free woman of color. Between the two women, he fathered six children. Even though Marie Jeanne Lemelle (–1803) was a slave, she had been certified by the Organization to be a mulatto, which was very important to Joseph. Their children were fmc Martin Gradenigo (1795–1850), fwc Henriette Gradenigo (1800–1882), and fmc Honore Louis Gradenigo (1801–1876). The children he had by fwc Adelaide Lemelle (1766–1828) were named fwc Aimee Lemelle Gradenigo (1796–1800), fwc Francois Gradenigo (1802–1833), and fmc Krebs Gradenigo (1813–). By the date of the wedding, both of Joseph Gradenigo's mistresses were dead. However, Joseph and his wife brought all the surviving children to the event so they could meet their relatives.

"Emilie Amilia's sister, Marie Genevieve Barre, widow of Daniel Telesphore Zeringue (1773–1829), came to the wedding with her children. Marie Genevieve and Daniel were married on September 13, 1802, in Pointe Coupee Parish. Their children's names were Daniel Telesphore Zeringue, Jr. (1804–1855), Honore Zeringue (1806–1855), Genevieve Zeringue (1809–), Charles Ovide Bienvenu Zeringue (1812–), Marie Arthemise Zeringue (1814–), Sosthenes Zeringue (1817–), Basile Zeringue, Telesphore Zeringue (1820–1884), and Marie Magdalena Zeringue (1823–1884). Honore Zeringue brought his wife, Adelaide (1810–), to the wedding along with their son, Honore Zeringue Jr. (1829–).

"Another sister, Euphrosine Barre, was with her spouse, John Close (1785–1865), and their children. Euphrosine and John were married in Opelousas, St. Landry Parish, on February 27, 1810. The names of the children were Charles Close (1811–1850), Joseph Hichee Close (1813–1844), Placide Zephirin Close (1813–1850), Euphrosine Close (1819–1863), Emily Close (1820–1892), Jean Pierre Close (1821–1860),

Genevieve Close (1822–1863), Elizabeth Close (1823–1888), Alexander Close (1825–1853), and Adolph Close (1831–1860).

"A deceased sister's children came. That sister's name was Julie Felicite Barre (1772–1830), and she had been married to Antoine Nezat dit Charpentier (1768–1823). They were married on New Year's Day in 1789, in Opelousas, St. Landry Parish. Their six surviving children were guests at the wedding. Their names were Alexis Nezat (1791–1856), Sophie Nezat (1793–1836), Marie Helene Nezat (1800–1861), Antoine Nezat (1803–1847), Arthemise Nezat (1806–), and Elenor Charpentier Nezat (1809–1870).

"Arriving with Alexis Nezat was his wife, Euphrozine Roy (1804–1850), a planter's daughter of St. Landry Parish. Alexis and Euphrozine were married on November 24, 1820, in Opelousas, St. Landry Parish. They brought their three children, Julie Marie Nezat (1822–), Alexis Nezat Jr. (1828–), and Euphrozine Nezat (1830–1888). The twenty-three-year-old Jean Baptiste Dejean (1808–1876) came with the family because he had a marriage contract for nine-year-old Julie Marie Nezat. Because of his age and his financial status, Jean Baptiste was not required to have his parents chaperone him to the wedding. However, young Julie Marie was always under the watchful eyes of either of her parents or her slave nanny.

"So far, I have told you about my grandparents, my uncles, my aunts, and their immediate families. But I have said little about the life of my father, Joseph Antoine DeCuir (1752–1822), the quintessential gentleman who lived all his life in Pointe Coupee Parish. My father loved women, especially colored women. But he never felt the need for marriage. Was this wrong on his part? Sorry, sir, but it is not my place or anyone's place to judge him. I consider him a man of his time.

"First, my father was born in wealth, and he never had to struggle for anything. The only hard thing he ever did was to fight in the American Revolutionary War. He and his brother Pierre DeCuir decided to enlist with General Bernardo de Galvez in his regiment. The French government was an ally of the thirteen English colonies in North America. The orders to General Galvez was to enlist enough men in a regiment that would prevent the English military from entering the Mississippi River by way of the Gulf of Mexico. If the English forces had free access to navigate north on the river, then they would be able to launch in attack from the west of the colonies in a surprise rear attack. Most importantly, if that were to happen, the English military would have made the colonies split their military and fight on two fronts.

"Thinking ahead, the French government looked at the big picture. If the English military were to win over the rebellious colonies, then nothing would stop the English from turning around and taking all of Louisiana from France. It was just a matter of whoever controlled the Mississippi River–controlled Louisiana. I must say that those Frenchmen and their friends fought very gallantly for the cause. My father said that they fought and won many skirmishes.

"Not only did they fight the English, but they also had to fight several battles with the Natchez and Chickasaw Indians. There were several reasons for the fight with the Natchez and the Chickasaw Indians. The English made those two tribes promises that were appealing to them. Promises were made to return all the lands that France took from them. Also, they promised that if they helped to defeat the thirteen rebellious colonies and their French allies from Louisiana, there would be no more encroachment on their lands by settlers from the east coast. Their final promise made to the two tribes was to become their ally in fighting their enemies, who were the Seminoles from the south and various Indian tribes from the north.

"After the American Revolutionary War ended in success for the Thirteen Colonies in 1784, General Galvez dispersed his army, and my father returned home to the DeCuir Plantation in Pointe Coupee Parish. His parents were now dead, and his siblings were living their lives successfully on their own plantations. He knew he needed feminine companionship. Since there were no white women available with class and since he had a special appetite for the Colored woman, my father made an appeal to the Organization for someone suitable for a man of his stature.

"The Organization consulted with the parents of fwc Marie Francoise de Beaulieu (1775–1812). Their names were Louis Chauvin de Beaulieu (1731–1801) and fwc Marianne Francour (1760–1810). Louis Chauvin de Beaulieu was born in Biloxi, French Louisiana Colony. These two had been married in Orleans Parish on February 16, 1770. The wife, fwc Marianne Francour, was born in Tchuopitaoulas, Orleans Parish.

"Do you have any more questions or concerns, sir? I believe I have told you everything about my family and how it became Colored," said the very tired Marie Claire.

"Ma'am!" said the young man. "You did not give me the pedigree or the background of your father's in-laws."

"Sir, the following pedigree was provided for Louis Chauvin de Beaulieu. His parents were Louis Chauvin Sieur de Beaulieu (1678–1729) and Charlotte Orbanne Duval (1710–1770). Both of them were born in Montreal, Quebec, Canada. They were married in 1724 in Quebec, and they arrived in the Louisiana Colony in the same year. Louis Chauvin Sieur de Beaulieu had French ancestry in that both of his parents had been born in France before they immigrated to Quebec. Their names were Pierre Chauvin (1631–1699) and Marthe Autreuil (1636–1713). Pierre was born in Anjou, Isere, Rhone-Alpes, France. Marthe was born in St. Germaine De Noyen Sur Sarthe, Angers, Anjou, France. I don't think anyone knows when Marthe left France to go to Montreal along with her family. But Pierre arrived in Montreal with his family in 1653. After a long supervised courtship, he married Marthe in Montreal on September 17, 1658. Both Pierre Chauvin and his wife, Marthe Autreuil, died in St. Francis Ille De Jesus, Quebec, Canada.

"I will take the time to tell you the names of Louis Chauvin Sieur de Beaulieu's siblings because I have an interesting tidbit to tell you. His siblings' names were Marie Marthe Chauvin (1662–1728), Pierre Chauvin Jr. (1663–1691), Jean Chauvin (1664–1667), Barbe Therese Chauvin (1665–1737), Giles Jules Chauvin (1668–1731), Michelle Chauvin (1670–1737), Jacques Chauvin Sieur de Charleville (1672–1732), Joseph Chauvin Sieur de Lery (1674–1732), Nicolas Chauvin Sieur de la Freniere (1676–1749), Paul Chauvin Sieur de Montpellier (1679–1699), and Jean Baptiste Chauvin (1681–1699)."

"Excuse me, madame," said the census taker. "If these persons shared the same parents, why did they have different surnames?"

"Well," Marie Claire explained, "let me briefly explain the situation to you. You see, Quebec did not have official titles for noblemen. But some men on various social strata such as merchants, explorers, teachers, and the like took to adding a superfluous title to their family names to sound important and to make an impression with people who were fascinated with noble sounding names. They made themselves *sieurs* or lords over fictitious places.

"There are three famous explorers from Quebec who most people are already acquainted. One was Rene Robert Cavelier Sieur de la Salle. The other two were the brothers, Jean Baptiste Le Moyne Sieur de Bienville and Pierre Le Moyne Sieur d'Iberville. Rene Robert Cavelier, who explored the Great Lakes areas, the Mississippi River, and the Gulf of Mexico and claimed the whole area for France, attached the name Sieur de la Salle to his family name of Cavelier so his name would carry a noble bearing. The two Le Moyne brothers, whom Louisiana and New Orleans will always be full of gratitude, also made themselves lords over fictitious places that were called Bienville and Iberville. Their family name was Le Moyne.

"So it was with five of the Chauvin brothers that Jacques made himself lord of Charleville. Joseph made himself lord of de Lery. Nicolas made himself lord of de la Freniere. Paul made himself lord of Montpellier. Of course, Louis made himself lord of de Beaulieu.

"One of Louis Chauvin's brothers, Nicolas Chauvin Sieur de la Freniere, received a 5,000-acre land grant from Jean Baptiste Sieur de Bienville as a reward for service in helping Bienville colonize Louisiana. He used it to settle his family on a plantation that he called Elmwood in 1762. It was located in what is now called Jefferson Parish on the River Road.

"After his death, the plantation was inherited by his son Nicolas Chauvin Sieur de la Freniere Jr. He became one of Colonial Louisiana's attorney generals. The younger La Freniere organized a revolt against Spanish rule in 1768, along with several like-minded French colonists. He was subsequently executed for his part in the conspiracy along with several of his companions on October 25, 1769. These patriots who were called traitors by the new Spanish government are immortalized in a street in New Orleans named for the martyrs. It was named Frenchmen Street. To honor the leader of the revolt, Nicholas Chauvin, the city eventually named Lafreniere Street after him. The 5,000-acre Elmwood Plantation was confiscated from the family by Spanish Governor Alejandro O'Reilly, also known as 'Bloody O'Reilly.' It was eventually occupied by the first American governor of Louisiana, William Charles Cole Claiborne. When Governor Claiborne lived on the site, it was a working plantation.

"The lady who became the wife of my grandfather, Louis Chauvin de Beaulieu, fwc Marianne Francour, was the daughter of two slaves. These slaves were of African descent and they did not speak English. They were taken together from their West African homeland. Marianne was born in Tchuopitaoulas, Orleans Parish. Through an interpreter, my grandfather Louis Chauvin de Beaulieu explained that he needed a wife. He explained that he would buy their freedom if they allowed him to marry their strikingly beautiful daughter. They knew he was rich and they were impressed he used the word 'marriage' and the word 'freedom.' They readily consented to a marriage contract."

"My grandfather bought her freedom first and married her. Soon afterward, he bought her parents' freedom. Louis and Marianne had these children: fwc Marie Nicolas Clemence Chauvin de Beaulieu (1763–1842), fmc Pierre Louis de Beaulieu (1765–1805), fwc Dorothee Chauvin de Beaulieu (1767–1809), fmc Joseph Chauvin de Beaulieu (1772–1819), fwc Marie Victoire Amedee de Beaulieu (1776–1868), and my dear mother, fwc Marie Francoise de Beaulieu (1775–1812).

"This is what I know of my African slave ancestors. They were traded into slavery by Africans. You know, a lot of people blame white people for enslaving Africans. This is not always true. Africans enslaved each other many, many hundreds of years before they ever saw a white man and his tall sail ship. The Africans, just like other men, always tried to increase their holdings in land, animals, and people. When the stronger tribe would defeat a weaker tribe, everything was confiscated from them, and the village was destroyed. The defeated people were taken and made into slaves. Anyone who resisted was killed.

"So, when the white traders arrived in Africa for the purpose of exchanging goods for slaves, they built their outposts on the coasts of Africa. The reason the white traders built their outposts on Africa's coast was that they were very afraid to go into the interior of Africa. I will remind you that the Western African slave trade began in the sixteenth century and ended before the middle of the nineteenth century. The Europeans did not have sophisticated weapons at the beginning of the African slave trade. Gun powder had been recently discovered from Asia, and it was hard to obtain. Therefore, their weapons were actually very crude and rudimentary. They had to bargain with the Africans rather than fight them because the Africans had the advantage of being on home ground.

"Africa at that time was called 'the dark continent' by white people because not much was known then about it. The Europeans relied on tales of large unknown man-eating animals, human-eating plants, and cannibals to form their opinions of that continent. What gave the already enslaved Africans more value to their African captors was that European ships carried on them items that appealed to the African chief and his people. These items which had little value to Europeans were things that the Africans did not grow or produce. Some examples of these items that appealed to the Africans' eyes were shiny, cheaply made necklaces, cloths, pots and pans, plates, forks, vests, pantaloons, and high hats.

"After the parents of my future mother, fwc Marie Francoise de Beaulieu, were properly financially compensated, as was the custom, for her hand, my father, Joseph Antoine DeCuir, whisked her away to the DeCuir family plantation. They lived the life as most wealthy planters did in splendid opulence, not having a care in the world. This couple had five children, fmc Antoine DeCuir (1788–1843), fwc Eugenie DeCuir (1790–1839), fmc Leufroy DeCuir (1794–1876), fwc Marie Celeste DeCuir (1795–1842), and of course me.

"Since my father was a veteran of the American Revolutionary War, he received a land grant from Congress after the Louisiana Purchase was completed in 1803. The land was located in Pointe Coupee Parish. This tract of land was on the west side of the Mississippi River, containing six arpents, four toise and one third front, and forty arpents in depth; and bound above by lands of the widow of his brother Pierre DeCuir and below by the widow of Charles Dufour. Since my father could now be independent from the DeCuir family land, he brought my mother and my siblings to his prized new land possession.

"The trouble with having so much land to me, was that it enabled my father, Joseph Antoine DeCuir, to have more than one woman and their children present at the same time with no one getting in anyone's space. Of course, my siblings and half-siblings knew each other, and we played together harmoniously daily. As for the three ladies, they were very cordial to each other because my father provided for them very well. Anyway, there is never a reason in polite society to be rude.

"My mother, fwc Marie Francoise de Beaulieu, was the eldest of my father's three ladies. The next oldest lady was fwc Henriette Labbe (1784–?). The youngest of the three was fwc Claire Louise Quevain (1795–1849). In fact, Claire lived longer than the other ladies, and she was able to take care of my father until his demise.

"Henriette Labbe was the daughter of Jean Labbe Jr. (1746–1793) and an unknown slave. Jean Labbe Jr. lived on the Labbe Plantation in New Roads, Pointe Coupee Parish. He was born there and had lived there all his life. Jean Labbe had a wife who was named Marie Francoise Barras (1753–1797). They were married on July 7, 1770, in Marie Francoise's hometown of St. Martinville, St. Martin Parish. Between the wife and the slave, Jean Labbe Jr. had ten children. My father's child by Henriette was named fmc Alphonse DeCuir (1805–).

"My half-brother, fmc Alphonse DeCuir, married once, and he also had another lady on his plantation. The lady in his life was fwc Marie Perrine Helene DeCuir (1815–). What I do know is that she was a DeCuir. But what I am unsure of is whether or not her lineage was part of my lineage. Be that as it may, she was part of my brother's entourage that attended the wedding. At the time of the wedding, she was only sixteen years old. Later the two of them had one child. His name was fmc Francois DeCuir (1834–).

"As was common practice, Alphonse decided to marry his niece when he was sixty-one years old and she was thirty-two years old, on March 16, 1866, in Pointe Coupee Parish. What was more remarkable about that marriage was not their family relationship, but it was her age.

Gosh! I really don't remember any other female in or out of the family that got married for the first time in their thirties. All of Helene's sisters were married when they were much younger. They were fwc Zeline DeCuir (1826–), fwc Angelina DeCuir (1834–), fwc Sofie DeCuir (1836–) and fwc Celine Zeline DeCuir (1840–). Of the sisters, Helene was usually spoken of as plain-looking and slow of speech. Usually, young girls were fully engaged with papers and an announcement of their engagement on the church's bulletin board by the time they were fifteen years old. The announcement would have two or more signed witnesses, and it would state their relationship to the bride and to the groom. Why, if a young lady was not engaged by the time she was nineteen years old, people would call her a spinster by the time that she was twenty years old. Therefore, I would be willing to lay odds that her inheritance from her deceased parents was so large that my brother was willing to forget how she looked so that he could greatly expand his holdings.

"Before I go any further, let me explain the family relationship between Alphonse and Helene. Alphonse was my brother because we shared the same father. Helene's parents were fmc Leandre DeCuir Sr. (1799–1838) and fwc Francoise Hopkins. Helene was born the same year that her father died. Thus, she never knew him. Leandre DeCuir's parents were fmc Antoine DeCuir Sr. (1788–1843) and fwc Sophie Deslonde (1779–1836). Antoine DeCuir Sr.'s parents were fmc Joseph Antoine DeCuir and fwc Marie Francoise de Beaulieu. Joseph and Marie Francoise were also my parents. So, Helene's father, Leandre was a nephew to my brother Alphonse and me because Leandre was the son of our brother Antoine. That's why I said from the beginning that my old brother Alphonse married his niece Helene. Alphonse and Helene had one child, a son, fmc Mederic Alexandre DeCuir (1866–).

"The parentage of fwc Claire Louise Quevain has remained unknown to me. It was somewhat of a mystery. I do know she was a beautiful dark-skinned lady whose hips rolled when she walked. Her disposition was appropriate to care for my father as he aged. He needed someone like her to have been able to put up with him. As he got older, he was very cranky and argumentative. He cussed a lot too. They had one child together. Her name was fwc Heloise DeCuir (1815–).

"Their daughter, fwc Heloise DeCuir, arrived to my daughter's wedding with her fiancé, fmc Severin Latapie Jr. (1814–). They were married soon after my daughter's wedding on May 6, 1832, in Pointe Coupee Parish. They were fortunate enough to have had seven children. Their names were fmc Jean Latapie (1836–), fmc Pierre Latapie (1838–), fwc Elise Latapie (1840), fwc Mary Latapie (1842–), fwc Marie Claire Latapie (1846–), fwc Teresa Latapie (1850–), and fwc Heloise Latapie. I don't know the birth or death information on Heloise.

"Severin Latapie Jr. was wealthy because he was the only heir to his deceased parents, Severin Latapie Sr., a wealthy white planter and fwc Marie Therese Cambrai. I don't remember their birth and death information. Severin Latapie Sr. received his land, as did so many of that time did, by being rewarded for special military duties for the French king. He kept a townhouse in New Orleans with his wife, child, and eleven household slaves. When not in New Orleans, they lived on their many acreage plantation in Pointe Coupee Parish. Marie Therese preferred country living because there were no social snobs in Pointe Coupee as it was in New Orleans. In New Orleans, she was not recognized as an equal partner in her relationship with Severin Latapie Sr. In fact, she could not attend the opera, the carnival balls, or house parties with him as her escort because of her color. But the most degrading thing that she had to do in New Orleans was to keep her hair covered.

"The Tignon Law of 1786, which was passed under the Spanish Governor, Don Estevan Rodriquez Miro was meant to keep the hair of all women of African descent covered at all times in Louisiana. The reason behind the law was that the few white women in the colony felt threatened by the hairstyles of the women of color. They thought that the manner of styles these colored women had with their hair and the way they decorated their hair with colorful beads, stones, and ribbons made them exotic looking creatures to their husbands and boyfriends. So, to protect their interests, they were able to influence men to pass the Tignon Law. Unfortunately for the white ladies, their plans to make the men ignore the women of color did not go as planned. The ladies of color were now more imaginative. With brightly covered fabrics, they invented so many attractive designs to wear that some became more intriguing and interesting looking and of course desirable to the white men."

EPILOGUE
THE CONCLUSION AND REFLECTIONS

"I hope, dear, that your questions about race mixing and culture of the colored people have been thoroughly answered by me. Just shake your tree, son—you never know who or what kind of people will fall out! Pardon me as I wipe a tear from my eye. I seem to tear up every time I talk about the ancestors and our glorious heritage. I miss those days just as I miss having money and someone to wait on me, hand and foot. I long for the respect that we had with the white people. I truly miss not having the changes of clothes made of quality materials that I use to wear. I am glad that my dear Papa and dear Mama are not here to see our despair.

"You see, young man, before the Civil War, Louisiana had three classes of people: White, Colored, and slave. The White and the Colored classes shared the same rights and privileges. After Louisiana became a state in 1812, the Americans tried to change our way of life. They did not understand the Colored people owning plantations and slaves. Of course, they did not understand our blood kinship with our White relatives and their respect of us. The Americans tried in the 1820s and the 1840s to pass laws to limit our rights. For example, one of their laws forbade us to own slaves. But we did!

"Now, it has been many years after the end of the Civil War, and our plight has changed. For example, there are now only two classes of people: White people and a combination of Colored people and former slaves that is called Negro. But for the Colored people, we will always call ourselves Creole. Our right to travel first class on the trains has been taken away. If we had money to conduct business in a bank, we now have to go to a rear door and see a bank employee in a dingy, low-lit back room. There have been other changes, and I really do not want to bore you with a list of things we can no longer do and places that we cannot go."

"Why, Miss Marie Claire," said the census taker "that sure does sound dreadful. I see you and your family here on a rich white man's land, working and hardly making it. Tell me please, whatever happened to your family and all the wealthy upper-class free Colored people who were high in society and attended your daughter's wedding?"

"The easiest thing that I can tell you is that once our land, money, assets, and social position were gone, we are barely scraping by," answered Miss Marie Claire. "The hardest thing to tell you is of the generations of our people who once lived in glorious splendor and who are now living in pitiful squalor. But I will tell you of what I remember and what I know so you can go on down the road to the next house."

"Why is it so hard for you to remember all the details?" inquired the census taker. "You seem to have done fine so far."

"Well, since the war ended, we just don't travel and have the kind of family and social gatherings we had before the war began. It was at these gatherings that we would catch up on births, marriages, baptisms, sicknesses, and deaths. I don't really know who is still alive," said Miss Marie Claire.

"As I relate to you about the families of which you inquired, you must remember two very important points of reference in our lives. There were the glorious times of our lives that were spent on plantations with our slaves and having all that we needed and most of our desires. Then, there was the time after the Civil War when our world crumbled. What I mean is that there is a difference in the lives of how the Creole people lived before the beginning of the Civil War and of those who were born after the war ended. These people never lived the extravagant and glorious lives that we did. They only know about it from the stories that we tell."

"I know that part is true," said the census taker. "I have gone all the way through the eighth grade, and I have never read of Colored people who lived opulent lifestyles as you have described to me."

Miss Marie Claire began by saying, "There are some of us who were able to join the new government in Louisiana as members of the Republican Party. One such person was fmc Antoine Dubuclet Jr. (1810–1887), who was married to my niece fwc Claire Pollard. He was elected as secretary of the treasury for the state of Louisiana. Then there were some who elected to live their lives as White people, and to this day, their children do not know that one or both of their parents are Colored people. I can tell you that the most common custom that repeated itself was close relatives marrying each other. Before the Civil War, the reason for doing so was to enlarge the family's wealth. Even now, the practice still prevails, and neither land nor wealth is involved. I believe that familiarity breeds attraction and love and that it just became a habit to marry your cousin and other such close relatives.

"Well, let me begin with the relatives that I remember. On February 26, 1836, in New Orleans, my cousin fwc Josephine Delphine Dubuclet (1816–) and my nephew fwc Antoine DeCuir Jr. (1816–1865) of Pointe Coupee Parish were married. Their son fmc, Antoine DeCuir III (1844–), married fwc Virginia Porche (1846–) in St. Landry Parish in 1866. Antoine and Virginia's son, fmc Francois Eugene DeCuir (1806–), and fwc Marie Blanche Trudeau (1862–) were married in 1887.

"Our cousins fmc Antoine Dubuclet Sr. (1773–1828) and his

wife, fwc Rosalie Belly (1785–1850), had a son, whose name was fmc Augustin Dubuclet (1819–1889). Augustin Dubuclet married fwc Marie Louise Ricard in St. Gabriel Catholic Church in Iberville Parish on January 29, 1846. Augustin and Marie Louise had a son, whose name was fmc Alexander Ludovic Dubuclet. On August 9, 1873, in Iberville Parish, fmc Alexander Ludovic Dubuclet (1847–) married fwc Marguerite Tolbert-Gonzales (1853–). They lived in St. Gabriel, Louisiana, Iberville Parish.

"The daughter of my brother, fmc Antoine DeCuir Sr., who was fwc Antoinette DeCuir (1826–) of Pointe Coupee Parish, married Arthur Edmund Denis (1823–). They exchanged their vows in New Orleans in the year of 1850.

"In Pointe Coupee Parish, my nephew fmc Leandre DeCuir Sr. (1799–1838) married fwc Francois Hopkins. Leandre was the son of my brother fmc Antoine DeCuir Sr. One of their daughters, fwc Zeline DeCuir (1826–), my niece, married fmc Jean Baptiste Tounoir III (1826–1869). Jean Baptiste Tounoir III is the grandson of Jean Baptiste Tounoir Jr., and my father's sister Marie Anne DeCuir. On April 27, 1854, my nephew, fmc Leandre DeCuir Jr., married fwc Flora Arlant (1836–1881). Leandre DeCuir Jr. and fwc Flora Arlant's daughter married my father's son, fmc Alphonse DeCuir (1805–), on March 16, 1866, in Pointe Coupee Parish.

"Married on February 7, 1888, were fmc Antoine Pollard Jr. (1841–) and fwc Mathilde Delphine Tounoir (1866–). Antoine Pollard Jr. is the grandson of my sister fwc Eugenie DeCuir and Louis Pollard II. My sister and her husband are also the great-grandparents of fwc Mathilde Delphine Tounoir.

"In 1839, fwc Lucille Tounoir (1825–) married fmc Arnaud Armand DeCuir (1816–1865). She married in a civil ceremony on her father's Arnaud Armand DeCuir Plantation in Pointe Coupee Parish. A priest was not available. Later in front of a priest on July 22, 1842, they were married in St. Francis Catholic Church in the same parish. Lucille Tounoir is the granddaughter of my father's sister Marie Anne DeCuir and Jean Baptiste Tounoir Jr. Arnaud Armand DeCuir is the son of my brother, fmc Antoine DeCuir Sr.

"On February 24, 1881, fmc Alexander DeCuir (1840–1890) was married to fwc Eugenie Armant (1855–). They were married in St. Francis Catholic Church in Pointe Coupee Parish. Alexander was the son of fmc Arnaud Armand DeCuir and fwc Lucille Tounoir.

"Armand and Lucille had a daughter, whose name was fwc Andorea DeCuir (1841–). She married fmc Emile Honore (1837–) on August 26, 1862. The site of this wedding was the mansion of the Arnaud Armand DeCuir Plantation in Pointe Coupee Parish. Emile Honore is the son of fmc Jean Francois Honore Destrehan Jr. (1811–1890) and fwc Euphemie Tounoir (1809–1847). Jean Francois Honore Destrehan Jr.'s parents were fmc Jean Francois Honore Destrehan Sr. and fwc Marie Celeste DeCuir (1795–), who was my sister.

"A sister of fwc Andorea DeCuir, fwc Marie Eusebie DeCuir (1846–1882), married fmc Jean Arthur Porche (1842–). Jean Arthur Porche had been born on his father's Zenon Porche Plantation in West Feliciana Parish. They exchanged their vows on July 30, 1872. The site of the wedding was on the home of fmc Armand Arnaud DeCuir in Pointe Coupee Parish.

"Another son of fmc Armand Arnaud DeCuir and fwc Lucille Tounoir was fmc Leon Villenueve William DeCuir (1850–). He married fwc Genevieve Adorea Ricard (1858–) in 1877. They were married in the home of her late parents, fmc Antoine St. Luc Ricard (1813–1873) and fwc Marie Leda Tounoir (1816–1872), which was located in St. Gabriel, Louisiana, Iberville Parish.

"Armand Arnaud and Lucille had a set of twins. Their names were fwc Rosalba DeCuir (1859–) and fwc Rosella DeCuir (1859–). First to get married was Rosalba to fmc Joseph Heleuter Ricard (1856–1888).

They were married on February 22, 1881. Then Rosella wed fmc Joseph Cleopha Porche (1860–) on February 16, 1886. Both of the weddings occurred in Raccourci, Louisiana, Pointe Coupee Parish.

"The Iberville Parish plantation of fmc Cyprien Ricard (1782–1826) and fwc Marie Genevieve Belly (1789–1825) was the site of the wedding reception for their daughter, fwc Delphine Antoinette Ricard (1813–1834). She married Antoine Ducoyet, a wealthy planter from Iberville Parish. Their wedding took place in St. Raphael Catholic Church in Bayou Goula, Iberville Parish.

"Delphine Antoinette's brother, fmc Lucien Ricard (1819–), married fwc Henriette Martin (1830–1861) on September 28, 1848. They married on the Iberville Parish plantation of Cyprien Ricard. This couple had three children who enjoyed the benefits of living on a plantation. These children were fmc Octave Ricard (1854–), fmc M. Ricard (1856–), and fwc Eugenie Ricard (1858–).

"The son of my sister, fwc Marie Celeste DeCuir (1795–) and her husband, fmc Jean Francois Honore Destrehan (1789–), whose name was fmc Jean Francois Honore (1811–1890), was married to fwc Euphemie Tounoir (1809–1847). They were married on February 18, 1840, in St. Francis Catholic Church in Pointe Coupee Parish.

"Jean Francois and Euphemie's son, fmc Martin Joseph Honore (1833–), married a gentle lady from New Orleans. Her name was fwc Marie Emesie N. Chesse (1844–). They were married in 1866 in her hometown.

"Another son, fmc Joseph Ovide Honore (1835–1886) married fwc Marie Estelle Ricard (1840–). They were married on December 29, 1859, in Brusly, Louisiana, Iberville Parish. Of the twelve children born to Joseph Ovide and Marie Estelle, three of them were born during the time the family lived lavishly on the Joseph Ovide Honore Plantation in Pointe Coupee Parish. These children were fwc Eugenie Honore (1860–), fmc Eugene Honore (1862–), and fwc Ledeiska Honore (1864–).

"On February 5, 1890, fmc Eugene Honore married fwc Eudora Purnell (1868–) in Raccourci, Louisiana, Pointe Coupee Parish. Eudora's parents owned the former Alexander R. Purnell Plantation in Morganza, Louisiana, Pointe Coupee Parish. Alexander R. Purnell, a free man of color, (1836–), was married to fwc Susan Rucker (1835–). He was the son of a former white plantation overseer who became a rich planter, Thomas R. Purnell (1798–1861), and fwc Mary Martin. Thomas R. Purnell was born in Maryland. He followed his employer to establish a plantation in Bayou Sara, West Feliciana Parish. His cabin on the plantation was next to the cabin of the slave Mary Martin. Because the owner of the plantation did not have any heirs and because Thomas R. Purnell had been a faithful and trustworthy employee, the owner bequeathed to Purnell all his worldly possessions, including the plantation and the slaves, when he passed away. Thomas R. Purnell, then, set Mary Martin free and married her. These were the humble beginnings of fmc Alexander R. Purnell.

"The daughter of fmc Joseph Ovide Honore and fwc Marie Estelle Ricard was married in 1884. Her name was fwc Ledeiska Honore (1864–). She married fmc Martin Alphonsus Honore (1854–).

"A son of fmc Jean Francois Honore and fwc Euphemie Tounoir, fmc Jean Omer Honore (1838–), wed fwc Marie Antoinette Ricard (1843–) on January 27, 1863. The site of the wedding was the Antoine St. Luc Ricard Plantation in Pointe Coupee Parish. Of their seven children, only one child, fmc Bonaparte Honore (1863–), enjoyed the luxurious life on a plantation.

"A daughter of fmc Jean Francois Honore and fwc Euphemie Tounoir, fwc Felicite Honore (1840–), married fmc Joseph Aristide Ricard (1834–). They were married on February 9, 1860, in St. Francis Catholic Church in Pointe Coupee Parish. She was welcomed by me into my family because she married my grandson. Joseph Aristide was the son of my late daughter, fwc Cydalise Celenie Porche (1816–1862) and her husband, fmc Pierre St. Luc Ricard IV (1805–1886). Felicite and Joseph Aristide had eleven children in nineteen years. Of the eleven children, four of them experienced life on the Jean Francois Honore Plantation. Those four children were fwc Elizabeth Ricard (1857–), fmc Dulac Ricard (1861–), fmc Joseph Israel George Ricard (1862–), and fmc Joseph Alcide Ricard (1864–). In 1885, this same fmc Dulac Ricard married fwc Rose Ricard (1862–) in Pointe Coupee Parish.

"A second daughter of fmc Jean Francois Honore and fwc Euphemie Tounoir, fwc Marie Leda Honore (1842–) married fmc Victor Duperon (1825–1868). He was a planter from the Duperon Plantation in Pointe Coupee Parish. They were married in their home parish on the Jean Francois Honore Plantation on December 2, 1862. Only one of their four children enjoyed the plantation lifestyle. Her name was fwc Marie Duperon (1865–).

"A third daughter was fwc Evelina Honore (1844–) who became the wife of fmc Victor Patin (1845–1890) on February 18, 1868, in Lakeland, Louisiana, Pointe Coupee Parish. This fmc Victor Patin was the son of fmc Celima Patin (1815–1867) and fwc Marie Celeste Honore (1823–1859). Marie Celeste was the daughter of my sister, fwc Marie Celeste DeCuir (1795–) and her husband, fmc Jean Francois Honore Destrehan (1789–).

"A third Honore son, fmc Jean Baptiste Honore (1847–1886), married fwc Eugenie Isabelle Patin (1848–). They were married on February 3, 1870, in Lakeland, Louisiana, Pointe Coupee Parish. Eugenie Patin was the daughter of fwc Marie Celeste Honore and fmc Celima Patin. Again, I must remind you that fwc Marie Celeste Honore was the daughter of my sister fwc Marie Celeste DeCuir and fmc Jean Francois Honore Destrehan.

"My sister fwc Marie Celeste DeCuir and her husband had another daughter whose name was fwc Jeanne Francoise Honore (1811–). She married fmc Martin Juge (1807–1872) in 1832. The wedding took place on the Jean Francois Honore Destrehan Plantation in Pointe Coupee Parish. After the wedding, the couple lived in their home parish on the Martin Juge Plantation. They had thirteen children during their marriage. Of the thirteen children, eleven enjoyed a splendid life on the Martin Juge Plantation. Their names were fwc Adelaide Juge (1833–), fwc Felicite Juge (1835–), fwc Celeste Juge (1836–), twins fwc Siles Juge (1838–) and fmc Martin Juge (1838–), fwc Euphemie Juge (1841–), fwc Marie Juge (1842–), fmc Francois Joseph Juge (1848–1872), fmc Charles Juge (1850–), fmc Joseph Emer Juge (1852–), and fmc Joseph Lefroir Antoine Juge (1855–).

"On December 22, 1866, fmc Martin Juge, Jr. married fwc Julie DeCuir (1847–1876) in Lakeland, Louisiana, Pointe Coupee Parish.

"Another son, fmc Francois Joseph Juge (1848–1872), married fwc Eugenie Pollard (1832–) on May 15, 1872. Eugenie Pollard was the granddaughter of my sister, fwc Eugenie DeCuir (1790–1839) and her husband, the wealthy planter Louis Pollard II (1770–1824).

"Another son of my sister, fwc Marie Celeste DeCuir, was fmc Zacharie Honore (1814–). He married fwc Marie Honore. They had nine children. Of these children, eight lived on the Zacharie Honore Plantation in East Baton Rouge Parish. The names of these children were fwc Henriette Honore (1846–), fmc J. Zacharie Honore (1849–), fwc Celeste Honore (1852–), fmc Martin Alphonsus Honore (1854–), fmc Abortpennier Honore (1858–), fmc Montphensier Honore (1859–), fmc Francois Honore (1862–), and fmc John V. Honore (1864–).

"In 1881, fmc Martin Alphonsus Honore married fwc Ledeiska Honore (1864–). They lived with their family in East Baton Rouge Parish.

"I do remember that one of my nieces had two wedding ceremonies. She was fwc Eugenie Honore (1818–), who was married twice to the same gentleman. She married fmc Francois Allain (1810–1865) first in a civil ceremony in December 1835. A ceremony was held before the justice of the peace because a priest was not available in this parish. At another time, one with a priest present was held in November 1842. They had six children, who were all members of a privileged class that owned thriving plantations. These six children's names were fmc Francois Alceste Allain (1837–1882), fmc Augustin Allain (1839–), fmc Jean Hubert Allain (1842–), fwc Marie Emelie Allain (1844–), fwc Marie Heloise Allain, and fwc Elvira Allain.

"About 1862, fmc Jean Hubert Allain and fwc Virginia Allain (1848–) were married. They lived on the Jean Hubert Allain Plantation in Pointe Coupee Parish. He inherited this plantation from his grandfather, the planter Francois Allain (1780–1850). They had one son of their five children who lived on the plantation with them. His name was fmc Honore A. Allain (1865–).

"My niece fwc Marie Celeste Honore and her husband, fmc Celima Patin, had five other children who lived with them on the Celima Patin Plantation in Lakeland, Louisiana, Pointe Coupee Parish. Their names were fwc Marie Celimen Patin (1846–1855), fwc Rosalie Patin (1852–), fmc Benoit Patin (1856–), fwc Marie Aline Patin (1858–), and fmc Joseph Hypolite Patin (1859–).

"On April 25, 1866, fwc Rosalie Patin (1852–) married fmc Matthieu Gatien DeCuir (1844–) in Lakeland, Louisiana, Pointe Coupee Parish. Their son fmc Benoit Patin (1856–) married fwc Josephine Dupas (1863–). Another daughter fwc Marie Aline Patin (1858–) married first to fmc Theodore Raphael Ricard (1855–). Theodore Raphael was my great-grandson. His grandmother was my late daughter fwc Cydalise Celenie Porche. For the second time, fwc Marie Aline Patin married fmc Joseph Israel George Ricard (1862–). On February 9, 1880, fmc Joseph Hypolite Patin (1859–) was married to fwc Eliska Ricard (1857–) in the Immaculate Conception Catholic Church in Lakeland, Louisiana, Pointe Coupee Parish.

"The youngest child of my sister, fwc Marie Celeste DeCuir was fwc

Marie Antoinette Adeline Honore (1824–). She married fmc Hypolite Porche (1825–) in 1839. They were married on the Jean Francois Honore Destrehan Plantation which was located in Morganza, Louisiana in Pointe Coupee Parish. Hypolite Porche was my son. Their seven children, my grandchildren, were born and raised on the Hypolite Porche Plantation which was located in Pointe Coupee Parish. Their names were fwc Marie Orphelia Porche (1843–1845), fmc Hypolite Porche Jr. (1844–), fwc Cleotine Porche (1845–), fwc Virginia Porche (1846–), fwc Felicite Porche (1849–), fmc Raymond Porche (1850–), and fwc Camille Porche (1852–).

"In 1866, fwc Virginia Porche, my granddaughter, married my nephew fmc Antoine DeCuir III. They were married in St. Landry Parish.

"My granddaughter, fwc Felicite Porche (1849–), first married fmc Joseph Alcide DeCuir (1843–1871). I do not remember the date of the wedding. After Joseph died, she married Charles Edgar 'Canon' Porche (1856–) in 1880.

"On February 22, 1870, my other granddaughter, fwc Camille Porche (1852–) married fmc Joseph Arthur Domingue (1842–) in Lakeland, Louisiana, Pointe Coupee Parish.

"Oh, let me not forget my dear cousin Jacques Philippe Charbonnet, Sr. (1770–1837) and his sweet wife, fwc Alexandrine Melanie Bernoudy (1783–1841). This is the same cousin Jacques who escaped with his entire family from the Charbonnet Plantation in St. Charles Parish during the slave uprising. Jacques was too ill to make the tedious trip to my daughter Cydalise's wedding. My cousin had ten children. These are the names of their children who lived with them on the plantation. They were fmc Jacques Philippe Charbonnet Jr. (1797–1877), fmc Jacques Pierre Charbonnet (1802–1823), fmc Louis Emilien Charbonnet (1804–1872), fwc Marie Melanie Charbonnet (1805–), fmc Francois Leo Charbonnet (1806–1865), fmc Pierre Adolphe Charbonnet

(1807–1872), fwc Alexandrine Charbonnet (1815–1873), fmc Adelard Evalture Charbonnet (1816–1860), fmc Philippe Bernard Charbonnet (1824–), and fwc Annette Charbonnet.

"On July 21, 1823, fmc Jacques Philippe Charbonnet Jr. married fwc Jeanne Anoie Daunoy on the Charbonnet Plantation in St. Charles Parish.

"During 1840, on the same site, fwc Alexandrine Charbonnet married fmc Gabriel Theodore Fazende (1810–1864). After their wedding, they resided on the Fazende Plantation in Plaquemines Parish with their children. The names of these children were fmc Lucien J Fazende (1841–), fmc Francois Leonce Fazende (1847–), and fwc Marie Alexandrine Fazende (1848–).

"Perhaps, sir, you would like for me to tell you about what happened to my Mayeux family?" asked Miss Marie Claire.

"Yes, I would like to know about your Mayeux cousins—if your tales do not last too long. I must leave soon," answered the census taker.

"I will try to cut it short then," she said.

"Remember, Antoine Mayeux (1798–1842) married fwc Rosalie (Rosalind) Broyard Barre June 24, 1817 on one of the Julien Etienne Broyard Barre Plantations in Avoyelles Parish. Their daughter, fwc Antoinette Mayeux (1820–1860), married Faustin Bordelon (1820–1880) in 1837. They were married on the Faustin Bordelon Plantation in Bordelonville, Avoyelles Parish. They had ten children who lived with them on the Faustin Bordelon Plantation. The names of these children were fwc Elmire Bordelon (1838–), fmc Paulin F. Bordelon (1839–1883), fmc Faustin Bordelon Jr. (1841–1883), fmc Jean Pierre D. Bordelon (1844–1870), fwc Cleophine Bordelon (1845–1870), fwc Celeste Eugenie Bordelon (1847–1870), fwc Aureline Bordelon (1851–1876), fmc Auguste Euchide Bordelon (1852–1860), fwc Roseline Flavie Bordelon (1854–), and fwc Marie Emma Bordelon (1856–).

"These are the marriages of the Bordelons. First married was fwc

Elmire Bordelon (1838–) to Evariste Paul Rabalais (1838–). They were married on August 28, 1856, on the Bordelon Plantation. After her husband's death, she married Dora Guillot (1832–), a former planter from Avoyelles Parish. They exchanged vows on November 7, 1867, in Avoyelles Parish. Second married was fmc Jean Pierre Bordelon (1844–1870), who married fwc Philomene Juneau (1841–) of Avoyelles Parish. Of their three children, two enjoyed the life of living on a plantation. Their names were fmc Alcide Desire Bordelon (1862–) and fwc Marguerite Sarah Bordelon (1865–). The third marriage was between fwc Cleophine Bordelon (1845–1878) and Jean Gajean (1834–), a planter from Avoyelles Parish. They married on May 19, 1864. The last person to get married on the Faustin Bordelon Plantation was fmc Paulin Bordelon (1839–1883) and fwc Estelle Rabalais. They were married on October 24, 1865. The war was over, and they soon lost their plantation and all their slaves. The last sibling married was fwc Celeste Eugenie Bordelon (1847–1870). She and John Thomas Walters, an American, were married on July 1, 1869, in Avoyelles Parish.

"Antoinette Mayeux's sister, fwc Emelie Mayeux (1819–1855) married Sosthene Alexander Couvillon (1814–1854). He owned his own plantation in Avoyelles Parish. They were married on her father's plantation in Avoyelles Parish on December 3, 1833. Their daughter fwc Evelina Couvillon (1837–) married her cousin Gervais Couvillon (1835–1861) on the Sosthene Couvillon Plantation on January 29, 1856. Their two children, fmc Jules Leonard Couvillon (1857–) and fmc Sosthenes Arcadius Couvillon (1860–), lived with them on the plantation. After her husband died, Emelie married Jean Despalangue (1837–) of Moreauville, Louisiana, Avoyelles Parish. They married on May 20, 1869.

"On April 30, 1859, Evelina Couvillon's sister, fwc Clementine Couvillon (1836–), married Jules Verdier (1830–1867) on his plantation in Mansura, Louisiana, Avoyelles Parish. After he passed away, she married her deceased sister's husband, Jean Despalangue, on December 10, 1877.

"Another sister fwc Luce Couvillon (1839–1868) married Evariste Aristide Gremillion (1831–) on May 12, 1859. They were married on the Martin Gremillion Plantation in Avoyelles Plantation. Three of their five children lived with them on the plantation. They were fwc Marie Rebecca Gremillion (1860–), fmc Oliver Chelbe Gremillion (1861–1865), and fwc Clemence Eudolie Gremillion (1864–).

"Their brother, fmc Edgard Couvillon (1843–), married fwc Flavie Bonnet Bonnette (1847–) on February 4, 1869, in Avoyelles Parish.

"Finally, their brother fmc Sosthenes Alexandre Couvillon Jr. (1848–1881), married fwc Irma Jeansomme (1853–1879) on December 17, 1868. They were married in La Chapelle de Choupique, Avoyelles Parish.

"Pardon me, sir, I am tired and hungry. I cannot think anymore," exclaimed Miss Marie Claire.

"Miss Marie Claire, it has been an honor to pause a while and to listen to your grandson and you. I have had the privilege of having my eyes opened wide by your most interesting stories of your endearing lives. I am too young to have witness all or even some of the things you have told me first hand. I only wish I could return home and tell others of what I have heard. They don't teach history properly in school! But under the present political climate in which we live, I dare not whisper a word of what you have revealed to me. I might lose my government-appointed job!"

The end

CPSIA information can be obtained
at www.ICGtesting.com
Printed in the USA
BVHW042341100323
660200BV00003B/6